# TRAINING ENGLISCH

Martin Paeslack

## Englisch 5. Klasse

Aufgaben mit Lösungen

Hauptschule

STARK

ISBN 978-3-86668-519-2

# Inhalt



*Fortsetzung siehe nächste Seite*

**Autor:** Martin Paeslack
**Illustrator:** Wolf Schröder

# Vorwort an die Schüler

**Liebe Schülerin, lieber Schüler,**

hörst du englische Musik und möchtest wissen, wovon die Texte handeln? Warst du schon einmal in einem englischsprachigen Land? Oder hast du in den Ferien jemanden kennengelernt, der kein Deutsch spricht, aber mit dem du dich auf Englisch verständigen konntest? Auch im Deutschen gebrauchen wir viele englische Wörter. So musst du dich in einem Fast-Food-Restaurant z. B. zwischen Milchshakes in den Größen „small", „medium" oder „large" entscheiden. Die englische Sprache begegnet dir also überall und es lohnt sich, sie zu lernen.

Die **Texte**, **Erklärungen**, **Beispiele und Übungen** in diesem Buch helfen dir dabei, dein **Grundwissen** im Fach Englisch zu trainieren. Wichtige Themen und Regeln, die du im Unterricht kennenlernst, werden auch hier behandelt.

- Jedes Kapitel beginnt mit einem **Text** und Aufgaben zum **Leseverstehen**. Die Texte handeln vom Alltag englischer Kinder in deinem Alter, die in der südenglischen Küstenstadt Eastbourne leben. Darüber hinaus wirst du einiges über die Weltstadt London und ihre Sehenswürdigkeiten erfahren.
- Es folgt jeweils eine kurze Erklärung zu einer **Grammatikregel** mit passenden Beispielsätzen. Du kannst diese Regel dann anhand einfacher und etwas schwierigerer Aufgaben üben.
- In jedem Kapitel findest du außerdem eine oder mehrere Übungen zu den Bereichen **Wortschatz** und **Schreiben**.
- Die **Lösungen** zu den Übungen findest du im „**Key**" am Ende des Buches.
- Du findest außerdem ein **Vokabelverzeichnis**, das dir diejenigen Wörter erklärt, die du nicht kennst oder die du vergessen hast. Du kannst damit aber auch deinen Wortschatz erweitern.

Du musst dieses Übungsbuch nicht ganz durcharbeiten. Du kannst auch immer an dem Kapitel arbeiten, das den Stoff beinhaltet, den ihr gerade im Unterricht behandelt. Oder du übst damit vor Proben bzw. Klassenarbeiten und wiederholst Kapitel, die dir Probleme bereiten. Eine weitere Möglichkeit wäre, das Buch zur Wiederholung von bestimmten Themen (z. B. „London") zu nutzen. Es ist auch sinnvoll, die Aufgaben nach einer Weile zu wiederholen, um festzustellen, ob du in bestimmten Bereichen noch fit bist.

Ich wünsche dir viel Spaß und Erfolg bei der Arbeit mit diesem Buch!

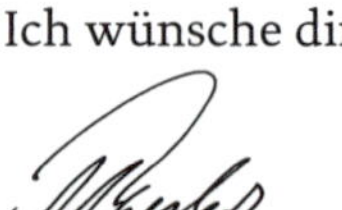

Martin Paeslack

# Vorwort an die Eltern

**Liebe Eltern,**

die fünfte Klasse ist für Ihr Kind ein wichtiges Jahr. Für viele Schülerinnen und Schüler ist es mit einem Neubeginn an einer anderen Schule verbunden und es werden die Grundlagen für ein erfolgreiches Englischlernen an der weiterführenden Schule gelegt. Mit diesem Buch kann Ihr Kind den Stoff der 5. Jahrgangsstufe im Fach Englisch selbstständig wiederholen und vertiefen.

- Der **gesamte Stoff dieses Lernjahres** wird verständlich erklärt und mithilfe von Beispielen veranschaulicht. Anhand von abwechslungsreichen **Aufgaben** können die jeweiligen Inhalte dann systematisch trainiert werden. Der Stoff richtet sich nach den aktuellen Lehrplänen der verschiedenen Bundesländer und ist damit breit gefächert.
- Die einzelnen Kapitel beginnen jeweils mit einem kleinen **Text**, der vom Alltag mehrerer fiktiver Schülerinnen und Schüler aus dem südenglischen Seebad Eastbourne handelt. Danach folgen Übungen zu den Kompetenzbereichen **Leseverstehen**, **Grammatik**, **Wortschatz** und **Schreiben**.
- Die Übungen beginnen auf einem einfachen Sprachniveau und werden dann zunehmend schwieriger. Zahlreiche **Bilder und Illustrationen** fördern den Lernprozess und bringen Freude beim Lernen.
- Ihr Kind sollte seine Antworten erst nach Bearbeitung einer Aufgabe mit den **Lösungen** im Lösungsteil („Key") vergleichen. Kennzeichnen Sie alles, was Ihrem Kind schwerfällt, damit Sie wissen, wo seine Schwächen liegen und worauf Sie bei der Wiederholung besonders achten müssen.
- Nicht nur das Erlernen der Sprachstruktur ist für Ihr Kind wichtig, sondern auch die Erweiterung seines **Wortschatzes** in der Fremdsprache. In diesem Buch kommen auch einige Wörter vor, die Ihr Kind noch nicht kennt. Damit wird trainiert, wie man die Bedeutung unbekannter Wörter mithilfe von Bildern oder aus dem Zusammenhang erschließt – eine Fähigkeit, die für den Gebrauch einer Fremdsprache unerlässlich ist. Außerdem findet sich am Schluss des Buches ein umfassendes **Vokabelverzeichnis** zum Nachschlagen und Wiederholen. So wird Ihr Kind zudem an den Umgang mit einem Wörterbuch herangeführt.

Ich wünsche Ihnen und Ihrem Kind viel Erfolg!

Martin Paeslack

# Topics and worksheets

In den folgenden Kapiteln findest du Texte mit Aufgaben zu unterschiedlichen Themen. Jedes Kapitel enthält Aufgaben aus den Bereichen Leseverstehen, Grammatik, Wortschatz und Schreiben. Du musst aber nicht alle Kapitel und alle Bereiche der Reihe nach durcharbeiten. Sieh einfach im Inhaltsverzeichnis nach, was du besonders üben möchtest.

# Topic 1: That's me

### Text 1: Tom

Hi, my name is Thomas Shaw.
All my friends call me Tom.
I'm eleven years old.

I'm from Eastbourne. It's a town in England. I live at 12, High Street.

My phone number is 01323 812357 and my e-mail address is tom2010@eastbourne.uk.

I go to Queen Anne's Comprehensive School in Eastbourne and I'm in Year 5. There are 25 pupils in my class. My teacher's name is Mrs Smith.

### Text 2: Catherine

Hi, my name is Catherine Smith.
I'm ten years old.

I'm from Eastbourne too.
I live at 57, Brighton Road.

My phone number is 01323 285620 and my e-mail address is cathy2000@eastbourne.uk.

I go to Queen Anne's School, too, and I'm also in Year 5. There are 21 pupils in our class and my teacher's name is Mr Jones.

## Fragen zum Text

**1** Lies den Text über Tom genau durch und kreuze die richtige Antwort an.

**a** Tom is from …
- ☐ Bournemouth.
- ☐ Eastbourne.
- ☐ Birmingham.

**b** His name is Tom …
- ☐ Sheldon
- ☐ Sharp
- ☐ Shaw

**c** He is …
- ☐ eleven years old.
- ☐ ten years old.
- ☐ twelve years old.

**d** His school is …
- ☐ Queen Elizabeth Comprehensive School
- ☐ Queen Anne's Comprehensive School
- ☐ Queen Annabel's Comprehensive School

**e** Tom is in …
- ☐ Year 4.
- ☐ Year 6.
- ☐ Year 5.

**f** His teacher's name is …
- ☐ Mr Smith.
- ☐ Mrs Smith.
- ☐ Mrs Jones.

**2** Lies den Text über Catherine und kreuze an, ob die Aussagen richtig *(right)* oder falsch *(wrong)* sind.

| | | right | wrong |
|---|---|---|---|
| **a** | Catherine is ten years old. | ☐ | ☐ |
| **b** | She is from London. | ☐ | ☐ |
| **c** | She lives in Brighton Road. | ☐ | ☐ |
| **d** | Her e-mail address is Catherine@england.uk. | ☐ | ☐ |
| **e** | She is in Year 7. | ☐ | ☐ |
| **f** | There are 25 pupils in her class. | ☐ | ☐ |

## Grammatik

**Welche Formen von *be* gibt es?**

Das Verb (Tunwort) *be* (sein) gibt es in zwei verschiedenen Formen: in der Langform und in der Kurzform. Im **gesprochenen Englisch** kommt die Kurzform öfter vor. Kurz- und Langform sind aber beide richtig.

| | Langform | Kurzform | |
|---|---|---|---|
| *1. Person Singular (Einzahl)* | I am nice. | I'm nice. | *Ich bin nett.* |
| *2. Person Singular* | You are nice. | You're nice. | *Du bist/Sie sind nett.* |
| *3. Person Singular* | He is nice. | He's nice. | *Er ist nett.* |
| | She is nice. | She's nice. | *Sie ist nett.* |
| | It is nice. | It's nice. | *Es ist nett.* |
| *1. Person Plural (Mehrzahl)* | We are nice. | We're nice. | *Wir sind nett.* |
| *2. Person Plural* | You are nice. | You're nice. | *Ihr seid/Sie sind nett.* |
| *3. Person Plural* | They are nice. | They're nice. | *Sie sind nett.* |

**3** Bilde ganze Sätze, indem du die richtigen Wörter verbindest. Manchmal gibt es auch mehrere richtige Lösungen.

| | | |
|---|---|---|
| he, you, she, it, they, I, you, we | is, am, are | Catherine Smith.<br>Queen Anne's School.<br>ten years old.<br>11 years old.<br>from England.<br>in Year 5.<br>Tom und Catherine.<br>from Eastbourne. |

**a** *I am ten years old.*

**b** You ______

**c** He ______

**d** She ______

**e** It ______

**f** We ______

**g** You ______

**h** They ______

**Wie bildest du die Verneinung von *be*?**

Wenn du einen Satz mit einer **verneinten Aussage** bilden möchtest, musst du eine Form von ***be* + *not*** einfügen:

| | Langform | Kurzform |
|---|---|---|
| *1. Person Singular* | I am not nice. | I'm not nice. |
| *2. Person Singular* | You are not nice. | You're not nice. |
| *3. Person Singular* | He is not nice. | He's not nice. |
| | She is not nice. | She's not nice. |
| | It is not nice. | It's not nice. |
| *1. Person Plural* | We are not nice. | We're not nice. |
| *2. Person Plural* | You are not nice. | You're not nice. |
| *3. Person Plural* | They are not nice. | They're not nice. |

**4** Vervollständige die Sätze mit der richtigen Verneinung von *be*.

**a** Tom ______________ from London. He is from Eastbourne.

**b** We ______________ happy about our new teacher. She is not nice.

**c** Tom and Catherine ______________ in Year 6. They are in Year 5.

**d** Tom is ill. He ______________ in school today.

**e** Catherine ______________ in the school bus.

**f** It ______________ a good lesson. It is boring.

**Wie bildest du Fragesätze mit *be*?**

Wenn du einen **Fragesatz** mit *be* bilden möchtest, steht statt des Personalpronomens eine Form von *be* am Satzanfang.

| | **Aussagesatz** | **Fragesatz** |
|---|---|---|
| *1. Person Singular* | I am (not) nice. | Am I (not) nice? |
| *2. Person Singular* | You are (not) nice. | Are you (not) nice? |
| *3. Person Singular* | He is (not) nice. | Is he (not) nice? |
| | She is (not) nice. | Is she (not) nice? |
| | It is (not) nice. | Is it (not) nice? |
| *1. Person Plural* | We are (not) nice. | Are we (not) nice? |
| *2. Person Plural* | You are (not) nice. | Are you (not) nice? |
| *3. Person Plural* | They are (not) nice. | Are they (not) nice? |

**Wie bildest du Kurzantworten zu Fragesätzen mit *be*?**

Die Wortstellung bei einer Kurzantwort entspricht derjenigen im Aussagesatz. Du musst dabei nicht den ganzen Satz wiederholen.

| | | |
|---|---|---|
| *Beispiele:* | Are you from London? | Yes, I am. / No, I am not. / No, I'm not. |
| | Is he from London? | Yes, he is. / No, he is not. / No, he isn't. |
| | Are they from London? | Yes, they are. / No, they are not. / No, they aren't. |

Die Kurzform von *be* kannst du dabei nur bei einer verneinten Kurzantwort verwenden.

**5** Mary und Matt aus Toms Klasse unterhalten sich. Vervollständige die Fragen und Antworten mit der richtigen Form von *be*.

__________ you in the theatre group?

Yes, I __________. __________ your phone number 23562117?

No, it __________. It is 85720569.

Do you know Catherine? __________ she nice?

Yes, she __________.

__________ Tom and Catherine friends?

Yes, they __________. __________ you and Tom in the basketball team?

No, we __________.

**Wortschatz**

**6** Catherine stellt ihren Freund Tom vor. Setze die folgenden Wörter an der richtigen Stelle im Text ein.

teacher address years phone number from pupils name are Year class

This is my friend. His __________ is Thomas Shaw. But all his friends call him Tom. He is eleven __________ old and he is __________ Eastbourne. It's a town in England. He lives at 12, High Street. His __________ __________ is 01323 812357 and his e-mail __________ is tom2010@eastbourne.uk. He goes to Queen Anne's Comprehensive School in Eastbourne and he's in __________ 5. There are 25 __________ in his __________. The name of his class __________ is Mrs Smith. Tom's hobbies __________ karate and rugby.

## Schreiben

**7** Ein englischer Freund/eine englische Freundin bittet dich, folgende Seite in seinem/ihrem Freundschaftsbuch auszufüllen.

Where are you from? ______________________

How old are you? ______________

What is your phone number? ______________________

What is your e-mail address? ______________________

What is the name of your school? ______________________

What year are you in? ______________

How many pupils are in your class? ______________

What's your class teacher's name? ______________________

# Topic 2: My friends

This is Trevor and Zoe.
I like them very much.
They are my best friends.
We do a lot of things together.

Trevor is in the school band.
He plays the guitar.
Trevor's mum comes from Germany.
So he also speaks German.

Zoe likes sports. She plays hockey in the school team and she also plays volleyball. Zoe is a very good dancer, too.

### Fragen zum Text

**8** Lies dir den Text genau durch. Ordne dann die folgenden Aussagen Trevor oder Zoe zu, indem du sie neben das richtige Bild schreibst.

"I can speak German."

"I play hockey in the school team."

"I like dancing."

"I play in the school band."

Trevor

___________________________________

___________________________________

___________________________________

___________________________________

___________________________________

___________________________________

Zoe

**9** Lies dir den Text über Trevor und Zoe noch einmal gut durch und kreuze an, ob die Aussagen richtig *(right)* oder falsch *(wrong)* sind.

| | | right | wrong |
|---|---|---|---|
| **a** | Catherine likes Zoe. | ☐ | ☐ |
| **b** | Trevor and Zoe aren't Catherine's best friends. | ☐ | ☐ |
| **c** | Trevor is in the football team. | ☐ | ☐ |
| **d** | He plays the piano, too. | ☐ | ☐ |
| **e** | Trevor's mum is from France. | ☐ | ☐ |
| **f** | Trevor can speak German. | ☐ | ☐ |
| **g** | Zoe likes sports. | ☐ | ☐ |
| **h** | She plays football. | ☐ | ☐ |
| **i** | She is in the school band. | ☐ | ☐ |
| **j** | Zoe isn't a good dancer. | ☐ | ☐ |

## Grammatik

**Was sind Personalpronomen (persönliche Fürwörter)?**

Ein Personalpronomen steht stellvertretend für eine Person oder Sache. Wenn das persönliche Fürwort das **Subjekt** (Satzgegenstand) eines Satzes ist, verwendest du folgende Formen:

| | | | |
|---|---|---|---|
| *1. Person Singular* | I *(ich)* | *1. Person Plural* | we *(wir)* |
| *2. Person Singular* | you *(du/Sie)* | *2. Person Plural* | you *(ihr/Sie)* |
| *3. Person Singular* | he, she, it *(er, sie, es)* | *3. Person Plural* | they *(sie)* |

**Wann verwendest du die Subjektform der Personalpronomen?**

- Die Subjektform der Personalpronomen kann ein Nomen (Namenwort) ersetzen, das Subjekt (Satzgegenstand) eines Satzes ist.

  *Beispiele:* Peter is nice. — He is nice.
  The house is big. — It is big.

- Im Englischen verwendest du im Singular (Einzahl) nur bei **Personen *he*** oder ***she*, sonst** benutzt du ***it***. Eine Ausnahme bilden Tiere, deren Namen du kennst. In diesem Fall gebrauchst du ebenfalls *he* oder *she*.

  *Beispiele:* The dog is beautiful. It is black.
  Bella is a beautiful dog. She is black.

**10** Tom und Catherine unterhalten sich. Setze das richtige Personalpronomen ein.

CATHERINE: ________ am in Year 5. Tom, are ________ in Year 5, too?

TOM: Yes, ________ am in Year 5. Do you know Mrs Smith? Is ________ your teacher?

CATHERINE: Yes, ________ is. Mr Jones, too. ________ are very good teachers.

TOM: What about Trevor? Are ________ friends?

CATHERINE: Yes, ________ are. ________ goes to Queen Anne's School, too. Are ________ in a school team?

TOM: Yes, ________ am. ________ play rugby. Are ________ in a school team, too?

CATHERINE: No, ________ am not. ________ sing in the school choir.

TOM: Oh, that's great. Let's go, ________ are late.

CATHERINE: Yes, ________ are right. Let's go!

**11** Vervollständige die Fragen und Antworten mit dem richtigen Personalpronomen und der richtigen Form von *be*.

**a** This is Catherine Smith.
__________ ten years old
and lives in Eastbourne.

**b** Tom Shaw isn't from London.
__________ from
Eastbourne, too.

**c** CATHERINE: Tom, how old __________?
TOM: __________ eleven years old.

**d** This is Trevor and Zoe.
__________ from
Queen Anne's School, too.

**e** Catherine likes Trevor and Zoe.
__________ her friends.

**f** Trevor plays the guitar. __________ in the school band.

**g** Zoe likes singing. __________ in the school choir.
__________ a good dancer, too.

**h** TOM: Hi, Catherine and Zoe. __________ in Mrs Miller's class?
CATHERINE and ZOE: No, __________. __________
in Mr Jones's class.

## Wortschatz

**12** Ergänze die Sätze mit einem passenden Wort. Die Bilder helfen dir dabei.

a Zoe has got a big ______________________.

b Trevor and Zoe are in Catherine's ______________.

c Catherine likes talking to her friends on the

______________________.

d Zoe's favourite subject is ______________________.

e Trevor likes going to the ______________________.

### Schreiben

**13** Nun beschreibe deine beste Freundin/deinen besten Freund. Die Vorgaben helfen dir. Schreibe in ganzen Sätzen.

My best friend's name ________________.

______ is from ________________.

It is a ______________ in ______________.

________________________ years old.

His/her phone ________________ is

________________________________.

His/Her e-mail ________________ is

________________________________.

My friend's hobbies ____________________________________________

________________________________________________________________

________________________________________________________________

I like my friend because ________________________________________

________________________________________________________________

________________________________________________________________

# Topic 3: My family

Tom and Catherine talk about their families:

### The Shaws

This is my family: my parents, Fred and Anita, and my two little sisters, Becky and Susan.

We live in a house with a big garden.

We have got three cats.
One cat, Miffy, is fifteen years old.
My sister Susan has got a dog.
Have you got a dog or a cat?

Tom's parents

Tom's sisters

Catherine's parents

Catherine's brothers

### The Smiths

Here is my family: my father, Brian, my mother, Michelle, and my brothers, David and Steven. They are twins and they are eight years old.
I haven't got a sister.

We live in a flat, but my grand-parents have got a big farm.
They have got hens and pigs. My grandmother has got a horse, too.

### Fragen zum Text

**14** Lies die Texte über Toms und Catherines Familien gut durch. Kreuze an, ob die nachfolgenden Sätze aus dem Text richtig *(right)* oder falsch *(wrong)* sind.

| | | right | wrong |
|---|---|---|---|
| **a** | Fred and Anita are Catherine's parents. | ☐ | ☐ |
| **b** | Fred and Anita have got three children. | ☐ | ☐ |
| **c** | The Shaws live in a house with a big garden. | ☐ | ☐ |
| **d** | The Shaws have got three dogs. | ☐ | ☐ |
| **e** | Catherine has got two little brothers. | ☐ | ☐ |
| **f** | They are eighteen years old. | ☐ | ☐ |
| **g** | Catherine has got a sister too. | ☐ | ☐ |
| **h** | Catherine and her family live on a big farm. | ☐ | ☐ |

**15** Lies den Text noch einmal genau durch. Ordne anschließend die folgenden Bilder Toms (T) oder Catherines (C) Familie zu.

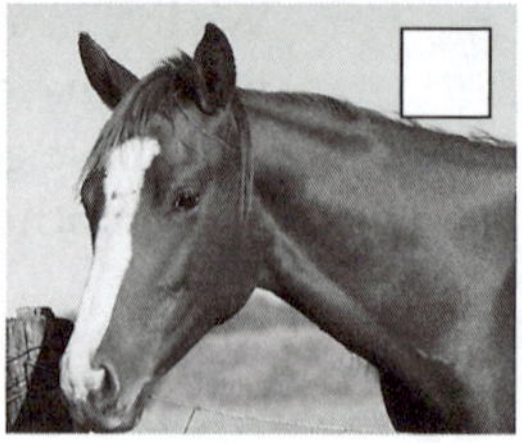

## Grammatik

**Wann verwendest du *have got/has got?***

*Have got/has got* verwendest du, um auszudrücken, was jemand **besitzt**.

**Welche Formen von *have got/has got* gibt es?**

Im **Aussagesatz** verwendet man folgende Formen:

| | **Langform** | **Kurzform** | |
|---|---|---|---|
| *1. Person Singular* | I have got | I've got | *ich habe* |
| *2. Person Singular* | you have got | you've got | *du hast/Sie haben* |
| *3. Person Singular* | he has got | he's got | *er hat* |
| | she has got | she's got | *sie hat* |
| | it has got | it's got | *es hat* |
| *1. Person Plural* | we have got | we've got | *wir haben* |
| *2. Person Plural* | you have got | you've got | *ihr habt/Sie haben* |
| *3. Person Plural* | they have got | they've got | *sie haben* |

*Beispiele:* I have got a sister. / I've got a sister. *Ich habe eine Schwester.*
He has got a sister. / He's got a sister. *Er hat eine Schwester.*

**Beachte:** Du kannst *have/has* auch ohne *got* verwenden.

**16** Becky und Susan erzählen von ihrer Familie. Setze die richtige Form von *have (got)* ein.

**a** Tom ________________ a red bike.

**b** He ________________ cool new shoes, too.

**c** We ________________ three cats.

**d** Susan ________________ a dog.

**e** Mum and Dad ________________ three children.

**f** They ________________ a beautiful house.

**g** The house ________________ a big garden.

**Wie bildest du die Verneinung von *have got/has got*?**

Wenn du einen Satz mit einer **verneinten Aussage** bilden möchtest, musst du ***not*** zwischen *have/has* und *got* einfügen. Meistens verwendet man die Kurzform.

| | **Langform** | **Kurzform** | |
|---|---|---|---|
| *1. Person Singular* | I have not got | I haven't got | *ich habe nicht* |
| *2. Person Singular* | you have not got | you haven't got | *du hast nicht/Sie haben nicht* |
| *3. Person Singular* | he has not got | he hasn't got | *er hat nicht* |
| | she has not got | she hasn't got | *sie hat nicht* |
| | it has not got | it hasn't got | *es hat nicht* |
| *1. Person Plural* | we have not got | we haven't got | *wir haben nicht* |
| *2. Person Plural* | you have not got | you haven't got | *ihr habt nicht/Sie haben nicht* |
| *3. Person Plural* | they have not got | they haven't got | *sie haben nicht* |

*Beispiele:* I have not got a sister. / I haven't got a sister. — *Ich habe keine Schwester.*
He has not got a sister. / He hasn't got a sister. — *Er hat keine Schwester.*

**Beachte:** Wenn du *have/has* ohne *got* verwendest, bildest du die Verneinung mit *do*:
I/you/we/ they do not have — I/you/we/they don't have
he/she/it does not have — he/she/it doesn't have

**17** Setze die richtige verneinte Form von *have (got)* ein.

**a** Catherine ______________________ a sister.

**b** Tom ______________________ a dog.

**c** Tom and his friend Lawrence ______________________ a football.

**d** Catherine ______________________ a hamster.

**e** The Shaws ______________________ a blue car.

**f** Mr and Mrs Smith ______________________ a house.

**g** They ______________________ a big garden.

**h** Catherine's grandmother ______________________ ten horses.
She has only got one horse.

**i** Catherine's grandparents ______________________ ponies.

**j** Catherine's grandfather ______________________ a dog.

**Wie bildest du eine Frage mit *have got/has got*?**

- Wenn du einen **Fragesatz** bilden möchtest, musst du *have/has* an den Anfang des Satzes stellen, wobei got an derselben Stelle wie im Aussagesatz bleibt.

| | **Aussagesatz** | **Fragesatz** |
|---|---|---|
| *Beispiele:* | You have got a little sister. | Have you got a little sister? |
| | *Du hast eine kleine Schwester.* | *Hast du eine kleine Schwester?* |
| | He has got a little sister. | Has he got a little sister? |
| | *Er hat eine kleine Schwester.* | *Hat er eine kleine Schwester?* |

- Bei **Kurzantworten** auf die Frage mit *have/has got* musst du *got* wegfallen lassen.

*Beispiele:* Have you got a little sister? — Yes, I have.
Has he got a little sister? — No, he hasn't.

- **Beachte:** Wenn du *have/has* ohne *got* verwendest, bildest du Fragen und Kurzantworten mit *do*:

*Beispiele:* Do you have a car? — Yes, I do. / No, I don't.
Does she have a car? — Yes, she does. / No, she doesn't.

**18** Catherines kleine Brüder stellen viele Fragen. Was wollen sie von Catherine wissen? Bilde die richtigen Fragesätze zu den Antworten.

**a** *Has Tom got two sisters? / Does Tom have two sisters?*

Yes, Tom has (got) two sisters.

**b** ______________________________

Yes, Mr and Mrs Shaw have (got) three children.

**c** ______________________________

Yes, Becky has (got) a new CD.

**d** ______________________________

No, Tom hasn't got/doesn't have a yellow bike.

**e** ______________________________

No, Becky and Susan haven't got/don't have new shoes.

**f** ______________________________

No, Mr Shaw hasn't got/doesn't have a new car.

## Wortschatz

**19** Hier siehst du Trevors Familie. Wie sind die einzelnen Familienmitglieder mit Trevor verwandt? Schreibe die englischen Bezeichnungen in den Stammbaum. Finde auch die Bezeichnungen für weitere Familienmitglieder heraus.

**Schreiben**

**20** Beschreibe Trevors Familie. Verwende dazu das Bild und die folgenden Informationen.

John Miller, 38

Kirsten Miller, 37

Amy Miller, 13

Trevor Miller, 11

John Miller is Trevor's ______________________________.

He is ____________ years old. Kirsten Miller is Trevor's ________________.

__________________________________________________

__________________________________________________

__________________________________________________

__________________________________________________

__________________________________________________

__________________________________________________

__________________________________________________

__________________________________________________

# Topic 4: My hobbies

Hello, my name is Trevor Miller.
I'd like to interview Tom Shaw and
Catherine Smith for our school newspaper.
Tom, what are your hobbies?

Hello, Trevor! I love sports. My favourite hobby is rugby. I play for our school team. I like karate and football, too. My favourite team is Chelsea. I don't like cricket because it's boring. I also play the guitar in a band. The name of our band is "The Friends". We play really cool music.

Oh, I play the guitar, too!
And now to you Catherine, what are your hobbies?

Hi, Trevor! Well, my favourite hobby is horse riding. I've got my own horse. Her name is Jewel. I often help my grandparents in their garden, too. I also love singing and listening to music. I play the violin and I sing in the school choir. My favourite singer is Miley Cyrus. She is great!

Catherine and Tom, thank you for the interview.

**Fragen zum Text**

**21** Welche Hobbys üben Catherine und Tom aus? Lies den Text genau durch und ordne die einzelnen Hobbys Tom oder Catherine zu, indem du Linien ziehst. Ein Hobby üben weder Tom noch Catherine aus.

**22** Lies dir den Text noch einmal durch und kreuze die richtige Antwort an.

**a** Tom's favourite hobby is …

- ☐ cricket.
- ☐ rugby.
- ☐ dancing.

**b** He also likes …

- ☐ skiing and football.
- ☐ karate and tennis.
- ☐ karate and football.

**c** Tom's favourite team is …

- ☐ Arsenal.
- ☐ Chelsea.
- ☐ the school team.

**d** Tom doesn't like …
- [ ] cricket.
- [ ] karate.
- [ ] tennis.

**e** Tom also plays the …
- [ ] trumpet.
- [ ] drums.
- [ ] guitar.

**f** Catherine's favourite hobby is …
- [ ] riding a bike.
- [ ] horse riding.
- [ ] playing games.

**g** Jewel is Catherine's …
- [ ] cat.
- [ ] horse.
- [ ] friend.

**h** Catherine often helps her grandparents …
- [ ] in the garden.
- [ ] in the house.
- [ ] in the kitchen.

**i** Catherine plays …
- [ ] the viola.
- [ ] the violin.
- [ ] the guitar.

**j** Catherine likes the music of …
- [ ] Tokio Hotel.
- [ ] The Friends.
- [ ] Miley Cyrus.

## Grammatik

**Was sind Possessivpronomen (besitzanzeigende Fürwörter)?**

Du benutzt Possessivpronomen, wenn du sagen möchtest, **wem** oder **zu wem etwas gehört**. Ein Possessivpronomen steht stellvertretend für eine Person oder Sache:

*Beispiel:* Is this Peter's bike? – Yes, it is his bike.
*Ist das Peters Fahrrad? – Ja, es ist sein Fahrrad.*

**Welche Possessivpronomen (besitzanzeigende Fürwörter) gibt es?**

| | | |
|---|---|---|
| *1. Person Singular* | my house | *mein Haus* |
| *2. Person Singular* | your house | *dein Haus / Ihr Haus* |
| *3. Person Singular* | his house | *sein Haus* |
| | her house | *ihr Haus* |
| | its house | *sein / ihr Haus* |
| *1. Person Plural* | our house | *unser Haus* |
| *2. Person Plural* | your house | *euer Haus / Ihr Haus* |
| *3. Person Plural* | their house | *ihr Haus* |

**Vorsicht:** Man kann einige Possessivpronomen leicht mit anderen Wörtern verwechseln.

*Beispiele:* its *(sein, ihr)* – it's *(es ist)*
their *(ihr)* – there *(dort)*
your *(dein / Ihr)* – you're *(du bist / ihr seid / Sie sind)*

**23** Verbinde die richtigen Sätze miteinander.

| | |
|---|---|
| **a** Tom and Catherine go to Queen Anne's School. | Its name is "The Friends". |
| **b** Miffy has got a basket. | It's their school. |
| **c** Trevor is in a band. | It's our hobby. |
| **d** I love Miley's music. | They are his hobbies. |
| **e** Tom likes karate and football. | It's her basket. |
| **f** We love singing. | She's my favourite singer. |

**24** Catherine und Tom sind im Wohnzimmer der Familie Smith. Setze jeweils das passende Possessivpronomen ein.

**a** CATHERINE: Look, Tom, this is __________ living room.

**b** TOM: Oh, __________ living room is big. Is this __________ video game? It's great.

**c** CATHERINE: No, it's __________ brother's video game. It's __________ new game.

**d** TOM: Here is __________ brother. Hi, Steven!

**e** STEVEN: Hi Tom, do you like __________ video game?

**f** TOM: Yes, I like it. Let's play __________ game!

**g** CATHERINE: Oh no, Tom! Let's go and ride __________ bikes.

### Wortschatz

**25** Lisa zählt ihre Hobbys auf. Vervollständige den Satz mithilfe der Bilder.

I play ______________________________________________

______________________________________________

______________________________________________

______________________________________________

## Schreiben

**26** Schreibe eine E-Mail an einen Brieffreund/eine Brieffreundin in England und erzähle, was du in deiner Freizeit gerne machst und was nicht.

Nachricht Einfügen Optionen Text formatieren

Senden

An...

Cc...

Betreff

Hi, ________________, *(Name deines Freundes/deiner Freundin)*

How are you? What is your favourite hobby?

My ______________________________________________

*(dein liebstes Hobby)*

I like it because ______________________________________

______________________________________________

______________________________________________

I also like ____________________________________________

______________________________________________

______________________________________________

*(deine anderen Hobbys)*

I don't like ____________________________________ because

______________________________________________

______________________________________________

*(Was machst du nicht gerne?)*

Write back soon!

________________ *(dein Name)*

## Topic 5: Catherine's room

It is 8.30 in the morning. Catherine is in her room with her mother. Mrs Smith is angry because Catherine's room is very untidy and Catherine is late for school.

CATHERINE: Mum, I can't find my new red pullover!
MRS SMITH: Well, your room is very untidy, but here is a green pullover.
CATHERINE: But I don't want a green pullover, I want the red pullover. I want to show it to Zoe at school.
MRS SMITH: Look under the bed, maybe the red pullover is there?
CATHERINE: Ah, there it is!
MRS SMITH: Do you need a T-shirt for sports?
CATHERINE: Yes, I need a T-shirt.
MRS SMITH: Here is the yellow T-shirt with the red stars. Is that OK?
CATHERINE: No, I want the white T-shirt!
MRS SMITH: The white T-shirt is in the washing machine. Catherine, don't be late for school!
CATHERINE: You are right. The yellow shirt is OK, Mum. I'm sorry. Bye, see you after school!

## Fragen zum Text

**27** Lies den Text über Catherine und ihre Mutter und kreuze an, ob die Aussagen richtig *(right)* oder falsch *(wrong)* sind.

| | | right | wrong |
|---|---|---|---|
| a | It's 8.30 in the evening. | ☐ | ☐ |
| b | Catherine is in the bathroom. | ☐ | ☐ |
| c | Mrs Smith isn't angry. | ☐ | ☐ |
| d | Catherine's room is very untidy. | ☐ | ☐ |
| e | Catherine can't find her green pullover. | ☐ | ☐ |

**28** Lies den Text noch einmal durch und kreuze jeweils die richtige Lösung an.

a Where is Catherine's pullover?

☐ ☐ ☐

b Catherine wants a …

☐ red T-shirt.
☐ white T-shirt.
☐ yellow T-shirt.

c But she can only have the …

☐ red pullover.
☐ yellow T-shirt with the white stars.
☐ yellow T-shirt with the red stars.

d The white T-shirt is …

☐ in the kitchen.
☐ in the washing machine.
☐ in the living room.

## Grammatik

**Wann verwendest du den unbestimmten Artikel (*a* oder *an*)?**

Du verwendest den unbestimmten Artikel (Begleiter) vor einem Nomen (Namenwort), wenn du von einer **nicht näher bestimmten Person oder Sache** sprichst.

*Beispiele:* a dog — *ein Hund* (also irgendein Hund und nicht ein ganz bestimmter)
an apple — *ein Apfel*

Der unbestimmte Artikel *a* bzw. *an* wird für Nomen im Singular (Einzahl) verwendet.

**Wie sprichst du den unbestimmten Artikel aus?**

- **Vor einem Konsonanten** (Mitlaut) wird der unbestimmte Artikel ***a*** verwendet.
  *Beispiel:* a car — *ein Auto*
- **Vor einem Vokal** (Selbstlaute: a, e, i, o, u) wird der unbestimmte Artikel ***an*** verwendet.
  *Beispiel:* an old tree — *ein alter Baum*

  Vor einem Wort mit einem *u* am Anfang, das [ju] gesprochen wird, wie z. B. *unit*, wird der unbestimmte Artikel *a* benutzt.

**29** Was wünscht sich Catherine zum Geburtstag? Ergänze die Sätze mit dem richtigen Wort. Die Bilder helfen dir dabei. Denke daran, den unbestimmten Artikel zu verwenden.

| book – mobile phone – animal – bike – ice cream |
|---|

Catherine would like to have …

a ______________________

b ______________________

c ______________________

d ______________________

e ______________________

**30** Setze in die folgenden Sätze den unbestimmten oder bestimmten Artikel ein.

Catherine has two brothers, but she doesn't have ______ sister. ______ names of her brothers are David and Steven. Catherine lives with her family in ______ flat, but her grandparents have got ______ house. ______ house is big. Catherine has got ______ best friend, Zoe. She is ______ very good dancer. ______ two girls, Catherine and Zoe, often go shopping.

### Wortschatz

**31** Tina und Tom waren shoppen. Benenne die einzelnen Teile, die sie gekauft haben, auf Englisch.

### Schreiben

**32** Schreibe zehn Kleidungsstücke auf, die du in deinem Schrank hast. Beschreibe das jeweilige Kleidungsstück (z. B. Farbe, Muster).

Beispiel: *I have (got) a green jacket.*

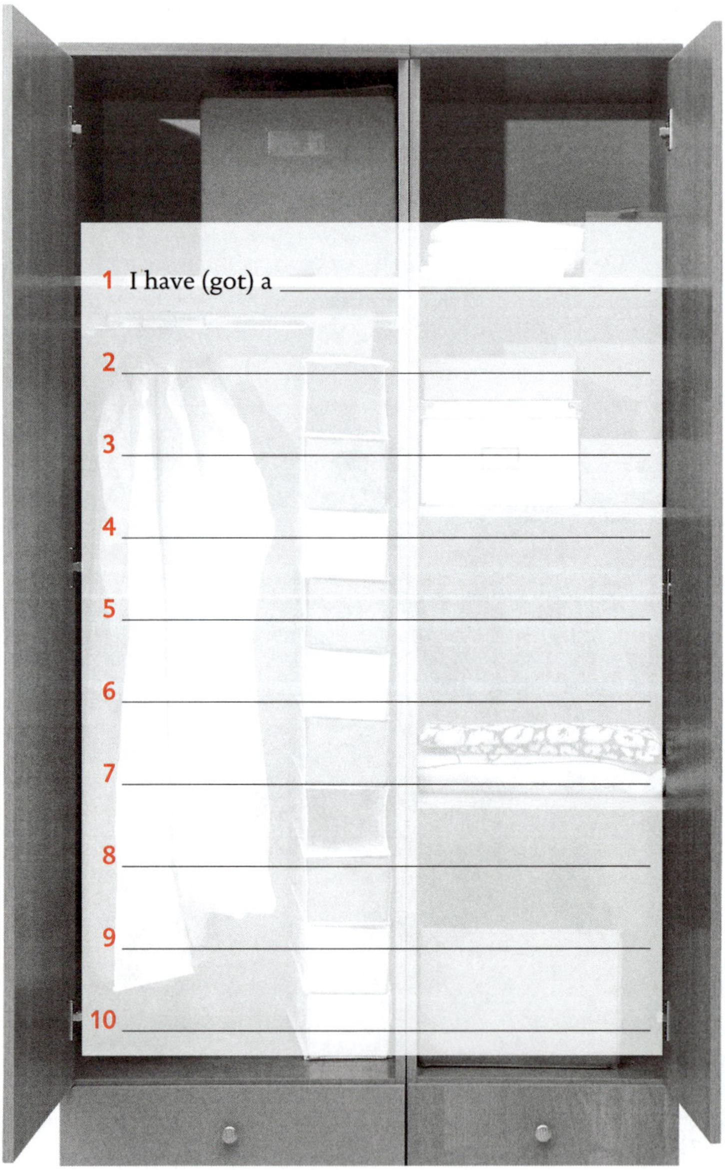

1 I have (got) a ________________

2 ________________

3 ________________

4 ________________

5 ________________

6 ________________

7 ________________

8 ________________

9 ________________

10 ________________

## Topic 6: Breakfast with the Shaws

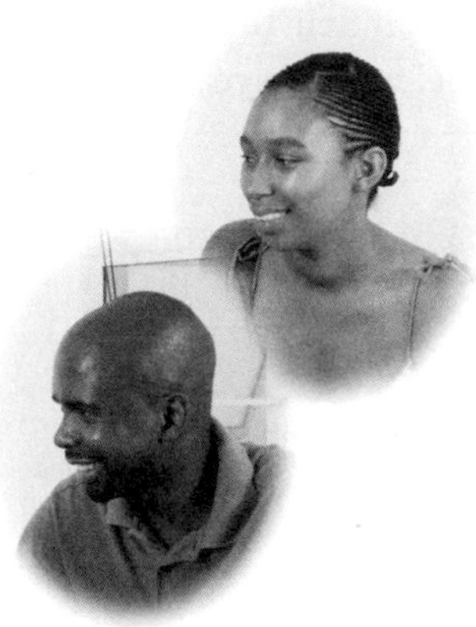

On Sundays the Shaw family always has an English breakfast with bacon and eggs, baked beans and toast.
Mr Shaw always has a cup of tea and two eggs.
Mrs Shaw has a slice of toast and a cup of coffee.
Tom eats baked beans with sausages and two slices of toast.
Tom's little sisters always eat cornflakes. They love chocolate cornflakes. Miffy, the cat, always drinks milk.

MR SHAW: Tom, can you pass me the honey, please?
TOM: Yes, here you are.
MR SHAW: Thank you, Tom.
BECKY: Mummy, can I have some more cornflakes, please?
SUSAN: Mum, I want more cornflakes, too! Becky, give me some of your cornflakes!
BECKY: No, you always want what I want!
MRS SHAW: Stop it! Here are some more cornflakes. There is enough for you.
BECKY: Thanks, Mum ... Here are your cornflakes, Susan.
SUSAN: Thank you, Becky. But you have got my spoon!
TOM: Oh, no! Little sisters!

## Fragen zum Text

**33** Lies dir den Text genau durch und vervollständige die folgenden Sätze. Ein Beispiel ist vorgegeben. Ein Satzende passt nicht.

| | |
|---|---|
| A Mrs Shaw | 1. … drinks tea. |
| B Mr Shaw | 2. … drinks milk. |
| C Tom | 3. … love chocolate cornflakes. |
| D Becky and Susan | 4. … drinks water. |
| E Miffy | 5. … eats baked beans with sausages. |
| | 6. … drinks coffee. |

| A | B | C | D | E |
|---|---|---|---|---|
| 6 | | | | |

**34** Lies den Text noch einmal durch und kreuze die richtige Antwort an.

**a** The Shaw family has an English breakfast on …
- ☐ Mondays.
- ☐ Saturdays.
- ☐ Sundays.

**b** An English breakfast has …
- ☐ baked eggs.
- ☐ bacon and eggs.
- ☐ chocolate cake.

**c** Mrs Shaw has …
- ☐ two eggs.
- ☐ a cup of toast.
- ☐ a slice of toast.

**d** Miffy is a …
- ☐ dog.
- ☐ cat.
- ☐ hamster.

**e** What does Mr Shaw like to have?

☐

☐

☐

**f** Becky wants to have more …

- ☐ milk.
- ☐ cornflakes.
- ☐ raspberry jam.

**g** Susan wants to have …

- ☐ a slice of toast.
- ☐ beans.
- ☐ cornflakes.

**h** Becky has Susan's …

☐ ☐ ☐

## Grammatik

**Wie bildest du den Plural (Mehrzahl)?**

- Bei den meisten Nomen (Namenwörtern) wird im Plural die Endung **-s** angehängt.
  *Beispiel:* one egg – two eggs
- An Nomen, die in der Einzahl auf *-s*, *-ch*, *-sh*, *-x*, *-ce* enden, musst du ***-es*** anhängen.
  *Beispiel:* one sandwich – two sandwiches
- Bei Nomen, die mit einem Mitlaut + -y enden, wird das -y zu ***-ie***.
  *Beispiel:* one hobby – two hobbies
- Es gibt auch einige unregelmäßige Pluralformen, die du auswendig lernen musst.
  *Beispiele:* one child – two children
  one man – two men
  one woman – two women

**35** Vervollständige folgende Sätze.

**a** Catherine normally has one sandwich for school, but today she has two ______________________ in her bag.

**b** One man is on the bike and two ____________ are in the car.

**c** Tom has one book in his bag and a lot of ____________ at home.

**d** London is a city in England. Munich and Hamburg are ______________ in Germany.

**e** Mr and Mrs Ratcliffe have one child. Mr and Mrs Shaw have three ______________________.

**f** One woman in the photo has got black hair, the other ______________ have got blonde hair.

**36** Schreibe das passende englische Wort im Singular und Plural unter jedes Bild.

______________________ ______________________ ______________________

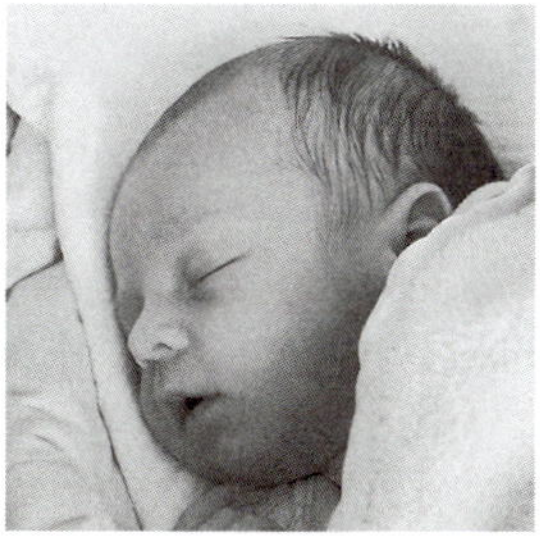

## Wortschatz

**37** Was kannst du auf dem Frühstückstisch der Shaws sehen? Schreibe die englischen Wörter in die richtigen Felder.

sausage – orange juice – coffee – egg – jam – bread – cheese – plate – cup – bacon

## Schreiben

**38** Schreibe auf, was du gerne zum Frühstück isst und trinkst und was du nicht magst. Wie sagst du es auf Englisch?

| Ich esse oder trinke gerne …<br>Ich mag …  | Ich esse oder trinke nicht gerne …<br>Ich mag kein(e) …  |
| --- | --- |
| | |
| | |
| | |
| • | • |
| • | • |
| • | • |
| • | • |
| • | • |
| • | • |
| • | • |
| • | • |

# Topic 7: A normal school day

Tom gets up. Then he takes a shower and has breakfast.

He leaves the house and takes the bus to school.

Tom arrives at school.

School starts.

Tom has a first break.

Tom has lunch in the school cafeteria.

Tom's school day ends. He takes the bus home.

On Tuesdays and Thursdays Tom has rugby training after school.

Tom has dinner with his family.

Then he does his homework and he often listens to music.

Tom goes to bed.

### Fragen zum Text

**39** Lies dir den Text über Toms Tagesablauf genau durch. Bringe dann die folgenden Sätze in die richtige Reihenfolge.

- **a** At 12 o'clock it is lunchtime.
- **b** In the evening he goes to bed at 9 o'clock.
- **c** Tom's school day ends at 4 o'clock.
- **d** In the evening Tom does his homework and he often listens to music.
- **e** Tom gets up at 7 o'clock in the morning.
- **f** At 8.15 he leaves the house and takes the bus to school.
- **g** He arrives at school at 8.45. School starts at nine o'clock.
- **h** Then he takes a shower and has breakfast.

| 1 | 2 | 3 | 4 | 5 | 6 | 7 | 8 |
|---|---|---|---|---|---|---|---|
| *e* | | | | | | | |

**40** Lies den Text über Toms Tagesablauf noch einmal. Beantworte dann die Fragen in ganzen Sätzen.

- **a** When does Tom get up in the morning?

  ______________________________

- **b** What does he do after that?

  ______________________________

- **c** When does school start?

  ______________________________

- **d** What does Tom do at 12 o'clock?

  ______________________________

- **e** At what time does school end?

  ______________________________

- **f** What does Tom do after school on Tuesdays and Thursdays?

  ______________________________

g What does Tom do before he goes to bed?

______________________________________________

h At what time does he go to bed?

______________________________________________

## Grammatik

**Wann verwendest du das *simple present*?**

Du verwendest das *simple present* (einfache Gegenwart) vor allem …

- wenn du ausdrücken willst, dass jemand etwas mag oder nicht mag.
  *Beispiel:* Peter likes his new bike. *Peter mag/gefällt sein neues Fahrrad.*
- wenn bestimmte Ereignisse regelmäßig stattfinden.
  *Beispiel:* I play football every Saturday. *Ich spiele jeden Samstag Fußball.*

  Zusammen mit dem *simple present* stehen oft Wörter und Ausdrücke, die dir sagen, **wie oft etwas geschieht**, zum Beispiel: *every day, sometimes, always, never, often*

  *Beispiel:* He gets up at 7 o'clock every day. *Er steht jeden Tag um 7 Uhr auf.*

**Wie bildest du das *simple present*?**

- Nach ***I / you / we / they*** behält das Verb (Tunwort) seine Grundform.
  Nach ***he / she / it*** wird an die Grundform die **Endung *-s*** angehängt.

| | | |
|---|---|---|
| *1. Person Singular* | I like the food. | *Ich mag das Essen.* |
| *2. Person Singular* | You like the food. | *Du magst das Essen./ Sie mögen das Essen. (Höflichkeitsform)* |
| *3. Person Singular* | He likes the food. | *Er mag das Essen.* |
| | She likes the food. | *Sie mag das Essen.* |
| | It likes the food. | *Es mag das Essen.* |

**Merke:** *He, she, it* – ***s*** muss mit!

| | | |
|---|---|---|
| *1. Person Plural* | We like the food. | *Wir mögen das Essen.* |
| *2. Person Plural* | You like the food. | *Ihr mögt das Essen./ Sie mögen das Essen. (Höflichkeitsform)* |
| *3. Person Plural* | They like the food. | *Sie mögen das Essen.* |

- **Beachte:** In der 3. Person Singular wird bei manchen Wörtern die Endung ***-es*** oder ***-ies*** angehängt:

  *Beispiele:* I do / he does
  I go / he goes
  I watch / she watches
  I carry / Peter carries

**41** Setze die richtige Form des *simple present* ein.

a Catherine and Zoe __________ (like) biology. It is their favourite subject.

b Tom ____________________ (love) his parents and his sisters.

c Tom and Trevor _______________ (meet) every Saturday.

d Trevor _________ (speak) a little bit of German.

e He always ____________________ (understand) the teacher's questions.

f Catherine _________ (do) her homework in the evenings.

g Catherine ____________ (go) to school first, then she ___________ (see) her grandparents.

**42** Was unternimmt Catherine jede Woche? Sieh dir ihren Terminplan an und vervollständige die Sätze.

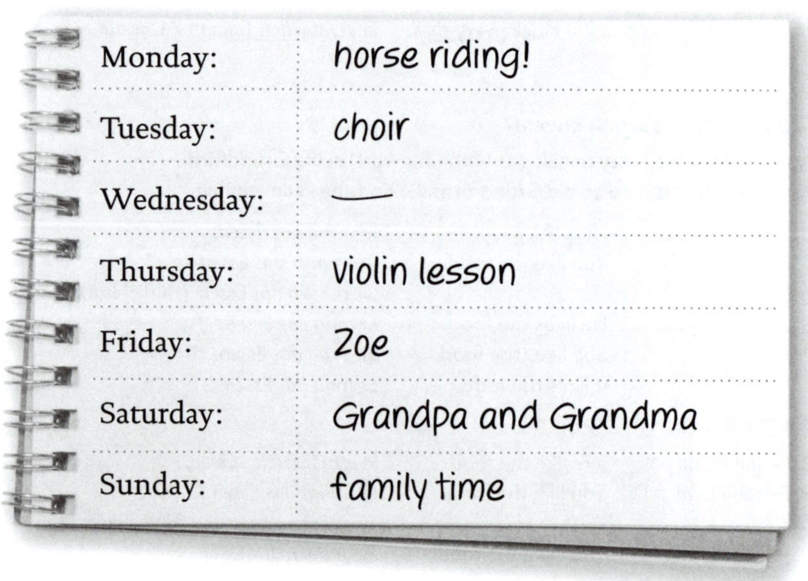


a On Monday Catherine ______________________________ (go) horse riding.

b On _______________________ she ___________________ (sing) in the choir.

c On ____________________________________________ (stay) at home and ______________________ (listen) to music.

**d** On ________________________________ (have) her violin lesson.

**e** On ________________________________ (meet) Zoe.

**f** On ________________________________ (help) her grandparents.

**g** On ________________________________ (do) something with her family.

**Wie bildest du verneinte Sätze im *simple present*?**

Nach ***I / you / we / they*** stellst du ***don't (do not)*** vor die Grundform des Verbs.
Nach ***he / she / it*** stellst du ***doesn't (does not)*** vor die Grundform des Verbs.

| | **Langform** | **Kurzform** |
|---|---|---|
| *1. Person Singular* | I do not go. | I don't go. |
| *2. Person Singular* | You do not go. | You don't go. |
| *3. Person Singular* | He does not go. | He doesn't go. |
| | She does not go. | She doesn't go. |
| | It does not go. | It doesn't go. |
| *1. Person Plural* | We do not go. | We don't go. |
| *2. Person Plural* | You do not go. | You don't go. |
| *3. Person Plural* | They do not go. | They don't go. |

**43** Bilde zu den folgenden Sätzen entweder die bejahte oder die verneinte Form des *simple present*. Die Bilder helfen dir dabei.

**a** Tom ______________ (go) to his rugby training every week.

**b** Catherine and Zoe ______________________ (play) football.

**c** Zoe ____________________ (sing) in a band.

**d** David and Steven __________________ (like) to do their homework.

e In the summer Steven ________________ (eat) ice cream every day.

f Trevor ________________ (play) the violin.

**Wie bildest du Fragen im *simple present*?**

- Bei Fragen mit ***I / you / we / they*** wird **Do** an den Anfang des Satzes gestellt:

| | **Aussagesatz** | **Fragesatz** |
|---|---|---|
| *Beispiele:* | You go swimming. | Do you go swimming? |
| | They like football. | Do they like football? |

- Bei Fragen mit ***he / she / it*** wird ***Does*** an den Anfang des Satzes gestellt. Im Fragesatz steht das Verb (Tunwort) dann in der Grundform (ohne -*s*).

| | | |
|---|---|---|
| *Beispiele:* | He goes swimming. | Does he go swimming? |
| | She likes football. | Does she like football? |
| | It looks good. | Does it look good? |

- **Kurzantworten** bildest du folgendermaßen: Personalpronomen + *do/don't* bzw. *does/doesn't*

| | | |
|---|---|---|
| *Beispiele:* | Do you like London? | Yes, I do. / No, I don't. |
| | Does she like London? | Yes, she does. / No, she doesn't. |

**44** Trevor interviewt seine Lehrerin Mrs Smith für die Schülerzeitung. Ergänze die Fragen und Kurzantworten mit der richtigen Form des *simple present*.

TREVOR: Good morning, Mrs Smith. Could I ask you some questions?
MRS SMITH: Of course, Trevor.

a TREVOR: ___Do you like___ being a teacher?
MRS SMITH: Yes, I ____________.

b TREVOR: ________ you ________ (have) a dog at home?
MRS SMITH: No, I ____________, I have a cat. Her name is Kitty.

c TREVOR: ________ she ________ (catch) mice?
MRS SMITH: No, she ____________.

**d** TREVOR: _________ you _________ (watch) TV? What is your favourite programme?

MRS SMITH: No, I _____________. So I don't have a favourite programme.

**e** TREVOR: _________ you _________ (have) a husband?

MRS SMITH: Yes, I _____________. His name is Francis Smith.

**f** TREVOR: _________ he _________ (teach) at a school?

MRS SMITH: No, he ________________. He is a doctor.

TREVOR: Thank you for the interview Mrs Smith.

MRS SMITH: Thank you, Trevor. Have a nice afternoon.

### Wortschatz

**45** Finde in der Wörterschlange diejenigen Wörter, die mit dem Thema „Schule" zu tun haben.

### Schreiben

**46** Fertige hier deinen Stundenplan auf Englisch an. Verwende das Wörterbuch.

| Time | Monday | Tuesday | Wednesday | Thursday | Friday |
|---|---|---|---|---|---|
| | | | | | |
| | | | | | |
| | | | | | |
| | | | | | |
| | | | | | |
| | | | | | |
| | | | | | |
| | | | | | |

**47** Wie sieht ein normaler Schultag bei dir aus? Schreibe über deinen Tagesablauf. Die Vorgaben und Zeichnungen helfen dir.

I get up ______________________ in the morning.

Then I ______________________.

At ______________ I leave the house and

______________________.

I arrive at school ______________.

School starts ______________. My first break is ______________.

Lunchtime is ______________. / We don't have lunchtime at school.

School ends ______________. Then I ______________.

After school I often ______________________.

In the evening I ______________________.

I go to bed ______________________.

# Topic 8: At home with the Shaws

Mr and Mrs Shaw both work and come home late. So Tom, Becky and Susan often help at home.

After dinner Tom and his father usually do the washing up and take out the rubbish.

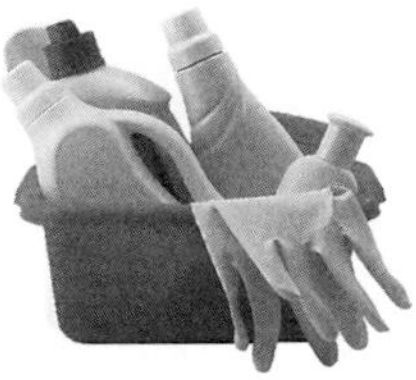

In summer Tom often waters the flowers in the garden.

Tom, Becky and Susan also tidy up their bedrooms every Saturday.

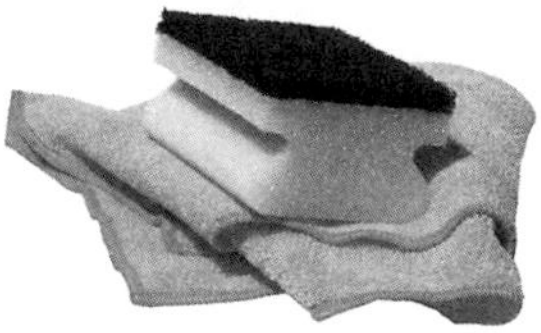

Becky always feeds Miffy, the cat.

Susan takes the family dog for a walk every day.

Tom doesn't like housework, but he always helps his parents. Mr Shaw sometimes gives him some money for his work. Then Tom usually goes to a music shop and buys a new CD.

### Fragen zum Text

**48** Lies dir den Text gut durch und schreibe dann auf, was die Aufgaben von Tom und seinen Schwestern sind.

**49** Lies dir den Text noch einmal genau durch und kreuze an, ob die Aussagen richtig *(right)* oder falsch *(wrong)* sind.

| | | right | wrong |
|---|---|---|---|
| **a** | Mr and Mrs Shaw come home early. | ☐ | ☐ |
| **b** | Becky and Susan don't tidy up their bedrooms. | ☐ | ☐ |
| **c** | Tom does the washing up after breakfast. | ☐ | ☐ |
| **d** | In summer Tom often waters the flowers in the garden. | ☐ | ☐ |
| **e** | Susan always feeds Miffy, the cat. | ☐ | ☐ |
| **f** | Becky takes the dog for a walk every day. | ☐ | ☐ |
| **g** | Tom doesn't like housework. | ☐ | ☐ |
| **h** | Mr Shaw sometimes gives Tom some money. | ☐ | ☐ |
| **i** | Tom usually buys clothes with the money. | ☐ | ☐ |

## Grammatik

**Wie sieht die Wortstellung im Englischen aus?**

Im englischen Aussagesatz gilt grundsätzlich folgende Reihenfolge:
**Subjekt** (Satzgegenstand) + **Prädikat** (Satzaussage) + **Objekt** (Satzergänzung).

| *Beispiel:* | Susie | does | her homework. |
|---|---|---|---|
| | Subjekt (S) | Prädikat (P) | Objekt (O) |

**50** Verbinde die einzelnen Satzteile und bilde sechs ganze, sinnvolle Sätze. Es kann dabei verschiedene Lösungen geben.

| | | |
|---|---|---|
| Becky | tidy up | her parents. |
| Tom and Trevor | waters | the flowers. |
| Becky and Susan | helps | the washing up. |
| Tom | feeds | new CDs. |
| Tom's father | buy | the cat. |
| Susan | does | their rooms. |

a ______________________________

b ______________________________

c ______________________________

d ______________________________

e ______________________________

f ______________________________

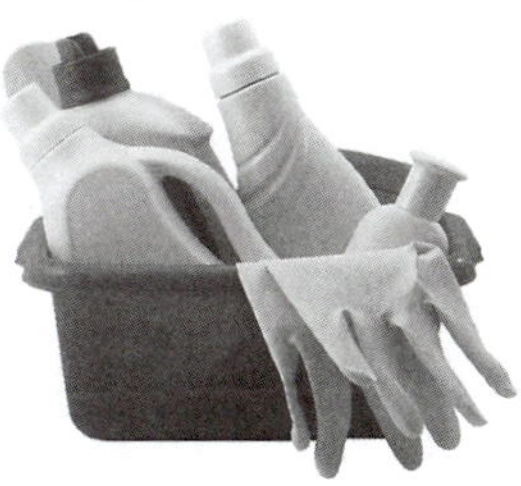

**Welche Adverbien (Umstandswörter) der Häufigkeit solltest du kennen?**
Hier sind die wichtigsten Adverbien der Häufigkeit. Sie beschreiben, **wie oft** etwas geschieht.

| | |
|---|---|
| always – *immer* | usually – *gewöhnlich, in der Regel* |
| often – *oft* | normally – *normalerweise* |
| never – *nie* | sometimes – *manchmal* |

*Beispiel:* I often go shopping. *Ich gehe oft einkaufen.*

**An welche Stelle im Satz stellst du die Adverbien der Häufigkeit?**
Die Adverbien der Häufigkeit stehen unmittelbar **vor** dem **Verb**:
*Beispiel:* Susie always does her homework.

**51** Bringe die folgenden Sätze in die richtige Reihenfolge.

a often – Tom – at home – helps

_______________________________________________

b the washing up – usually – Tom and his father – do

_______________________________________________

c the cat – Becky – feeds – always

_______________________________________________

d every day – takes the dog for a walk – Susan

_______________________________________________

e gives – Mr Shaw – Tom – sometimes – some money

_______________________________________________

f to a music shop – goes – usually – Tom

_______________________________________________

## Wortschatz

**52** Hier siehst du das Haus der Shaws. Ordne die unten angegebenen Wörter den Ziffern zu.

| roof – door – garden – window – garage |
|---|

1. ____________________
2. ____________________
3. ____________________
4. ____________________
5. ____________________

**53** Hier siehst du Toms Zimmer. Ordne die Wörter den Gegenständen zu.

| chair – bed – lamp – bookshelf – desk – floor |
|---|

**54** Welche Tätigkeiten gibt es im Haushalt? Ergänze die Mindmap mit den unten angegebenen Wörtern.

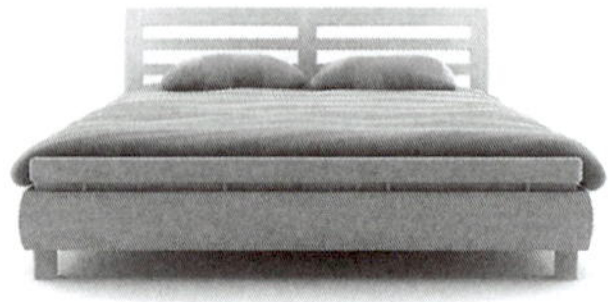

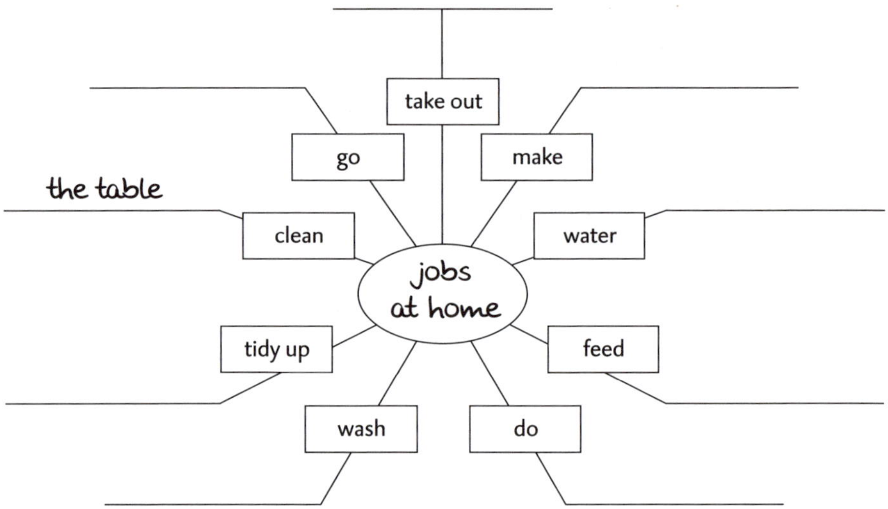


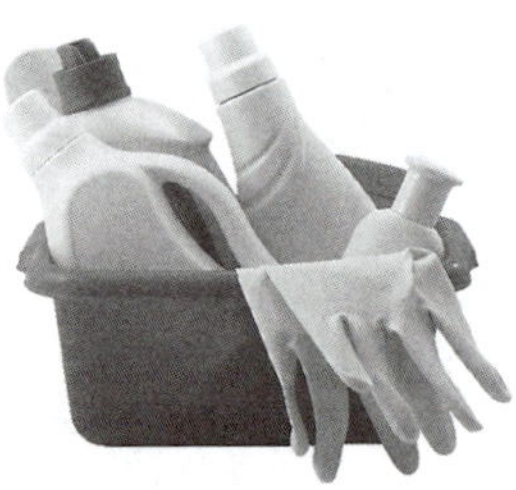

Füge die folgenden Wörter ein:

washing up bedroom flowers rubbish bed ~~table~~ cat shopping car

## Schreiben

**55** Welche Arbeiten müssen die Shaws heute erledigen? Sieh dir die Zettel auf der Pinnwand der Familie Shaw an. Schreibe auf, was die einzelnen Familienmitglieder machen müssen.

**a** Susan has to ______________ in the ______________.

**b** Tom ______________________________ his room.

**c** Anita ______________________________.

**d** Becky ______________________________.

**e** Fred ______________________________.

## Topic 9: At school with Zoe

It's ten o'clock in the morning. Catherine and her friend Zoe are in their classroom. Catherine has got a large school bag. There are a lot of things in the bag: A ruler, a felt tip, her school books, her exercise books, an eraser and some food. But where is her pencil case?

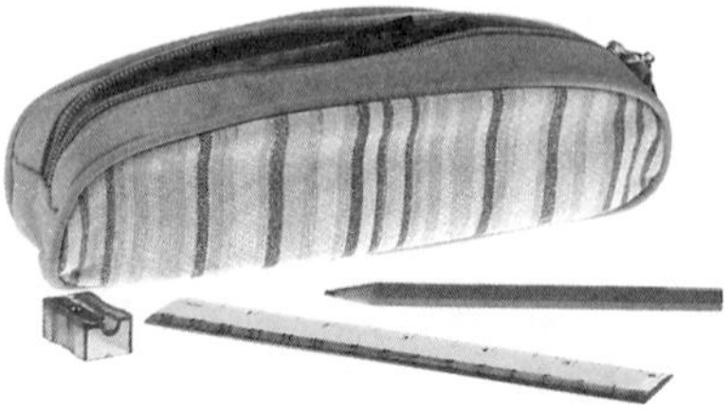

ZOE: Hi Catherine, how are you? Why are you so nervous? What's wrong?
CATHERINE: Oh Zoe, I can't find my pencil case. Where is it? Do you have it?
ZOE: No, Catherine, I don't have it and I don't know where it is. Where can it be? Is it still in your bag?
CATHERINE: No, it isn't. Is it under the desk? Have a look please, Zoe.
ZOE: No, it isn't. Is it behind the blackboard?
CATHERINE: Ha ha, but maybe next to the chair on the floor?
ZOE: No, but look in front of the window! There's a pencil case.
CATHERINE: That isn't my pencil case. That pencil case is blue and my pencil case is green.
ZOE: Look in your school bag again … There it is!
CATHERINE: Oops, I'm sorry, Zoe.
ZOE: No problem, Catherine. You always look for something. But when does the next lesson start?
CATHERINE: In two minutes. Who is our new teacher?
ZOE: Mrs Ratcliffe.
CATHERINE: Oh, that's great. I like her.

### Fragen zum Text

**56** Lies dir den Text genau durch. Entscheide, ob die Aussagen richtig *(right)* oder falsch *(wrong)* sind. Verbessere den Satz, falls die Aussage falsch ist.

| | | right | wrong |
|---|---|---|---|
| a | Catherine and her friend Zoe are at home.<br>*Catherine and Zoe are at school/in their classroom.* | ☐ | ☑ |
| b | Catherine's school bag is empty.<br>________________________________ | ☐ | ☐ |
| c | Catherine can't find her pencil case.<br>________________________________ | ☐ | ☐ |
| d | The pencil case isn't under the desk.<br>________________________________ | ☐ | ☐ |
| e | Catherine's pencil case is blue.<br>________________________________ | ☐ | ☐ |
| f | Catherine's pencil case is in her school bag.<br>________________________________ | ☐ | ☐ |
| g | Catherine doesn't like Mrs Ratcliffe.<br>________________________________ | ☐ | ☐ |

**57** Lies den Text noch einmal gut durch und vervollständige dann die folgenden Sätze. Versuche, die Aufgabe zu lösen, ohne auf den Text zu sehen.

a "Hi Catherine, ________ are you? ________ are you so nervous? What's wrong with you?"

b "Oh Zoe, I can't find my pencil case. ________ is it?"

c "No, Catherine, I don't have it and I don't know ________ it is. … ________ it still in your bag?"

d "That pencil case is blue and __________ pencil case is green."

e "____________ in your school bag again … ________ it is!"

f “But ____________ does the next lesson start?”

g “In two ________________. ________ is our new teacher?”

## Grammatik

**Wie heißen die Fragewörter im Englischen?**
Hier ist eine Liste wichtiger Fragewörter im Englischen:

| | | |
|---|---|---|
| What? *(Was?)* | Why? *(Warum?)* | Where? *(Wo?)* |
| Who? *(Wer?)* | How? *(Wie?)* | When? *(Wann?)* |

**Wann verwendest du Fragen mit *what*?**

- Mit *what* fragst du nach **Dingen** oder nach etwas, das gerade geschieht.
  *Beispiele:* What would you like to eat? *Was möchtest du gerne essen?*
  What is she doing? *Was macht sie gerade?*
- Mit *what* gibt es auch einige **feststehende Ausdrücke**, die du am besten auswendig lernst:
  *Beispiele:* What is her name? *Wie heißt sie?*
  What time is it? *Wie spät ist es?*
  What colour is it? *Welche Farbe hat es?*

**58** Stelle zu folgenden Antworten Fragen mit dem Fragewort *what*.

a Question: *What is your name?*
Answer: My name is Tom.

b Question: ______________________________
Answer: It’s 5 o’clock.

c Question: ______________________________
Answer: The bike is red.

d Question: ______________________________
Answer: I would like to drink an orange juice.

e Question: ______________________________
Answer: I can see a house.

**Wann verwendest du Fragen mit *who*?**

Du verwendest ***who***, wenn du wissen willst, **wer** etwas tut. *Who* bezieht sich immer auf **Personen**.

*Beispiele:* Who is in the house? *Wer ist im Haus?*
Who can play football? *Wer kann Fußball spielen?*
Who writes e-mails? *Wer schreibt E-Mails?*

**59** Bilde zu den jeweiligen Antworten passende Fragen mit dem Fragewort *who*.

**a** Question: *Who is in the classroom?*
Answer: Catherine and Zoe are in the classroom.

**b** Question: ______________________
Answer: Catherine has got a big school bag.

**c** Question: ______________________
Answer: Catherine is nervous.

**d** Question: ______________________
Answer: Zoe sits next to Catherine.

**e** Question: ______________________
Answer: Catherine always looks for something.

**f** Question: ______________________
Answer: Zoe finds the pencil case.

**g** Question: ______________________
______________________
______________________
Answer: Mrs Ratcliffe is the new teacher.

**Wann verwendest du Fragen mit *where*?**

Du verwendest ***where***, wenn du wissen möchtest, **wo** sich eine Person oder eine Sache befindet, oder wenn du wissen möchtest, **woher** jemand kommt.

*Beispiele:* Where is Peter? — *Wo ist Peter?*
Where are the Shaws from? — *Woher sind die Shaws?*

**60** Sieh dir die folgenden Bilder an und bilde dazu Fragen mit *where* sowie die dazugehörigen Antworten. Die folgenden Ausdrücke helfen dir dabei:

on the table – in the supermarket – in the garden – in the car

**a** Question:
Where are ______

Answer:
______

(books?)

**b** Question:
______

Answer:
She is ______

(Zoe?)

**c** Question:
______

Answer:
______

(Trevor?)

**d** Question:
______

Answer:
______

(Tom?)

**Wann verwendest du Fragen mit *how?***

Mit dem Fragewort **how** (wie) gibt es einige häufige Wendungen, die du dir merken solltest:

| | | |
|---|---|---|
| *Beispiele:* | How are you? | *Wie geht es dir?* |
| | How old is Zoe? | *Wie alt ist Zoe?* |
| | How much is the book? | *Wie viel kostet das Buch?* |
| | How many books do you read? | *Wie viele Bücher liest du?* |

Zum Gebrauch von *much* und *many* siehe Topic 16, Seite 103.

**61** Formuliere die Fragen auf Englisch.

a Frage jemanden, wie es ihm/ihr geht.

_______________

b Frage jemanden, wie viel Geld er/sie hat.

_______________

c Frage jemanden, wie viele Brüder er/sie hat.

_______________

d Frage jemanden, wie alt er/sie ist.

_______________

e Frage jemanden, wie viele CDs er/sie hat.

_______________

**Fragen mit *why?***

Du gebrauchst das Fragewort **why** (warum), wenn du wissen willst, was der **Grund** für etwas ist. Auf *why*-Fragen folgt immer eine **Antwort mit *because*** (weil).

| | | |
|---|---|---|
| *Beispiel:* | Why do you like Tom? | I like Tom because he's nice. |
| | *Warum magst du Tom?* | *Ich mag Tom, weil er nett ist.* |

**62** Stelle Fragen mit *why* oder antworte mit *because*.

a Question: Why do you like your birthday?

Answer: *I like my birthday because* I always get presents.

**b** Question: Why are you happy?
Answer: ______________________ it is my birthday.

**c** Question: ______________________?
Answer: I walk home because I haven't got a bike.

**d** Question: Why can't you see the cat?
Answer: ______________________ under the table.

**e** Question: ______________________?
Answer: I like Zoe because she is nice.

**Wann verwendest du Fragen mit *when*?**
Du gebrauchst das Fragewort **when** (wann), wenn du nach einem bestimmten **Zeitpunkt** fragst.
*Beispiele:* When is the shop open? *Wann ist das Geschäft geöffnet?*
When can I see you? *Wann kann ich dich sehen?*

**63** Stelle Fragen mit *when* und beantworte sie in ganzen Sätzen. Die Vorgaben helfen dir dabei.

**a** Question: (school over)
*When is school over?*
Answer: (4 o'clock)
*School is over at 4 o'clock.*

**b** Question: (do homework)
______________________
Answer: (afternoon)
______________________

**c** Question: (your birthday)
______________________
Answer: (May)
______________________

**d** Question: (supermarket open)
______________________
Answer: (8 o'clock)
______________________

**e** Question: (play rugby)
______________________
Answer: (on Thursdays)
______________________

## Wortschatz

**Was kannst du mit Präpositionen (Verhältniswörtern) ausdrücken?**

Präpositionen sind Wörter, mit denen du unter anderem ausdrücken kannst, **wo Dinge sind.**
Lerne die hier angegebenen, häufig gebrauchten Präpositionen des Ortes auswendig.

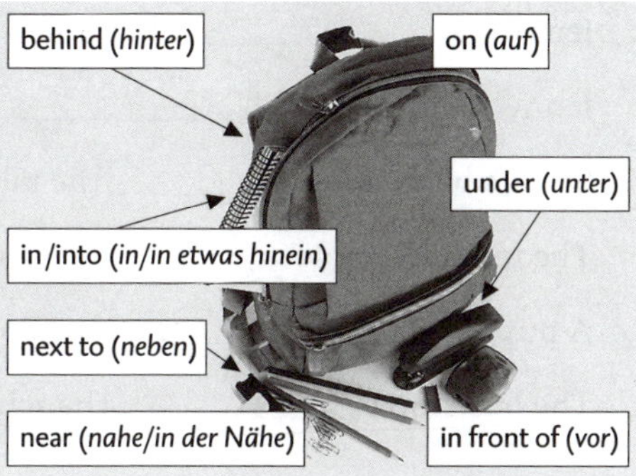


**64** Sieh dir das Bild an und vervollständige die nachfolgenden Sätze mit den richtigen Präpositionen aus dem obigen Kasten.

- **a** The pupils are ______________ the classroom.
- **b** Jenny sits ______________ her friend Sarah.
- **c** Jenny's schoolbag is ______________ the table.
- **d** Sarah's book is ______________ the table.
- **e** The teacher's table is ______________ the blackboard.
- **f** A pupil is ______________ the blackboard.
- **g** The bus stop is ______________ the school.

### Schreiben

**65** Beschreibe, welche Dinge du am Abend in deine Schultasche packst.
So kannst du beginnen:

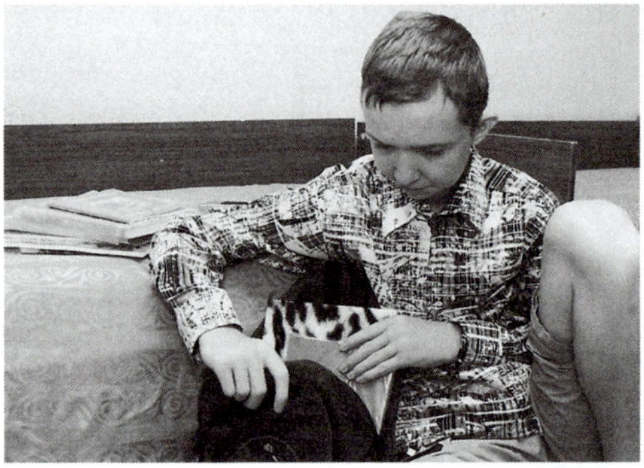

I put ______________________________________________ in my school bag.

Then ______________________________________________

______________________________________________

______________________________________________

______________________________________________

______________________________________________

______________________________________________

______________________________________________

______________________________________________

## Topic 10: In town

It is 10 o'clock on a Saturday morning. Tom, Catherine and their friends Trevor and Zoe meet at the town centre near the station. They want to go to the Eastbourne Lifeboat Museum. It is a museum about ships and the sea.

TOM: Hi, Catherine and Zoe. How are you?
ZOE: I'm fine.
CATHERINE: Me, too. Where is Trevor?
TOM: He's in the computer shop. But here he is!
TREVOR: Hi, Catherine and Zoe. Let's go to the Lifeboat Museum now. Where is it?
CATHERINE: I don't know. Let's ask the policeman. Excuse me, Sir, where is the Lifeboat Museum?
POLICEMAN: Go along Gildredge Road. Turn left onto South Street. Go straight on. Turn right into Devonshire Place. Then turn right again onto Grand Parade. Go straight on. The Lifeboat Museum is on the left on King Edward's Parade.
CATHERINE: Thank you, Sir. Let's go.

Ten minutes later the friends are at the Lifeboat Museum. They are in the museum the whole day because it is very interesting.

When they leave the museum, they decide to go to Eastbourne Pier. They buy cokes and sandwiches and sit down on the beach. It is a warm day. Trevor and Tom take off their shoes and socks and run into the water.

CATHERINE: Be careful, boys!

Suddenly Tom slips on a stone and falls into the water. He is wet all over. Trevor laughs and helps Tom to stand up again.

CATHERINE: That's Tom! Now we have to go home.

## Fragen zum Text

**66** Lies den Text genau durch und kreuze die richtige Antwort an.

**a** When do Tom, Catherine and their friends meet?

 ☐  ☐  ☐

**b** They meet on a …
- ☐ Sunday morning.
- ☐ Saturday morning.
- ☐ Saturday afternoon.

**c** The friends meet …
- ☐ at a computer shop.
- ☐ near the station.
- ☐ near the stadium.

**d** The Lifeboat Museum is about …
- ☐ fish in the sea.
- ☐ ships and the sea.
- ☐ chips and computers.

**e** Who do the friends ask for help?

☐  ☐ 

☐ 

**f** The Lifeboat Museum is in …
- ☐ King Edward's Parade.
- ☐ Grand Parade.
- ☐ Devonshire Place.

**g** The museum is …
- ☐ boring.
- ☐ funny.
- ☐ interesting.

**h** Tom slips on …

☐ a crab. ☐ a stone. ☐ his shoe.

**67** Zeichne auf der Karte den Weg ein, den der Polizist beschreibt.

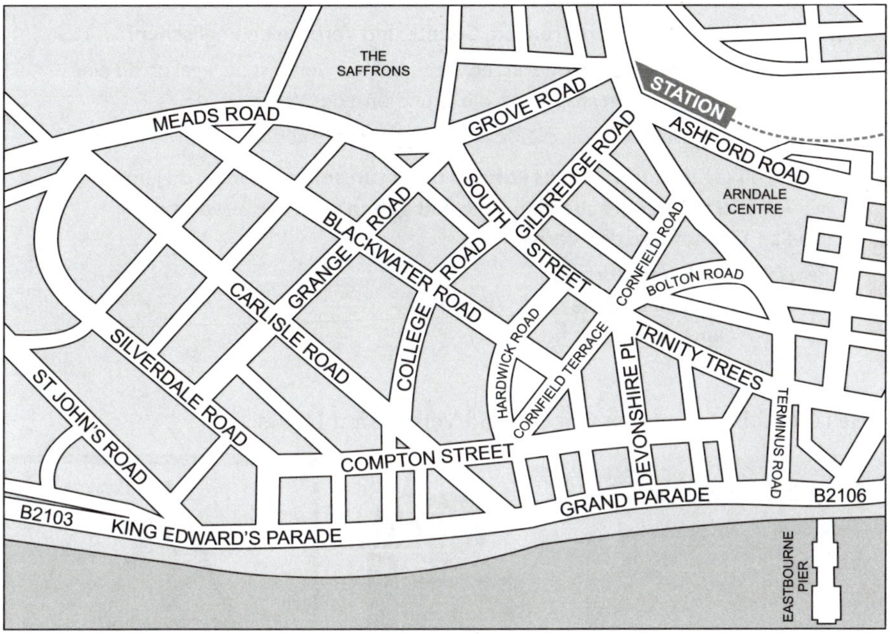


**68** Bringe die folgenden Sätze in die richtige Reihenfolge. Vergleiche deine Lösung anschließend mit dem Text.

| | | |
|---|---|---|
| A | I'm fine. | |
| B | Hi, Catherine and Zoe. Let's go to the Lifeboat Museum now. Where is it? | |
| C | Me, too. Where is Trevor? | |
| D | Go along Gilredge Road. Turn left onto South Street. Go straight on. Turn right into Devonshire Place. Then turn right again onto Grand Parade. Go straight on. The Lifeboat Museum is on the left on King Edward's Parade. | |
| E | I don't know. Let's ask the policeman. Excuse me, Sir, where is the Lifeboat Museum? | |
| F | Thank you, Sir. Let's go. | |
| G | Hi, Catherine and Zoe. How are you? | 1 |
| H | He's in the computer shop. But here he is! | |

## Grammatik

**Wie formulierst du Aufforderungen, Gebote und Verbote im Englischen?**

- Wenn du **jemanden aufforderst**, etwas zu tun, verwendest du, egal ob du eine oder mehrere Personen ansprichst, die Grundform des Verbs.

  *Beispiel:* Give me the book, please. *Gib mir bitte das Buch.*

- Wenn du sagen möchtest, **was jemand nicht tun soll**, oder wenn du jemanden vor etwas **warnen** oder aber ihm einen **Rat geben** willst, verwendest du ***Don't* + Grundform des Verbs**.

  *Beispiele:* Don't run! *(Befehl)*
  Don't play on the road! *(Warnung)*
  Don't drink it, it's hot. *(Rat)*

**69** Wie lauten die folgenden Gebote und Verbote auf Deutsch?

## Wortschatz

70 Beschrifte die einzelnen Gebäude und Orte der Stadt. Schreibe die Bezeichnungen jeweils in die grauen Kästen.

## Schreiben

**71** Vervollständige Toms E-Mail an seinen Austauschpartner in Deutschland.

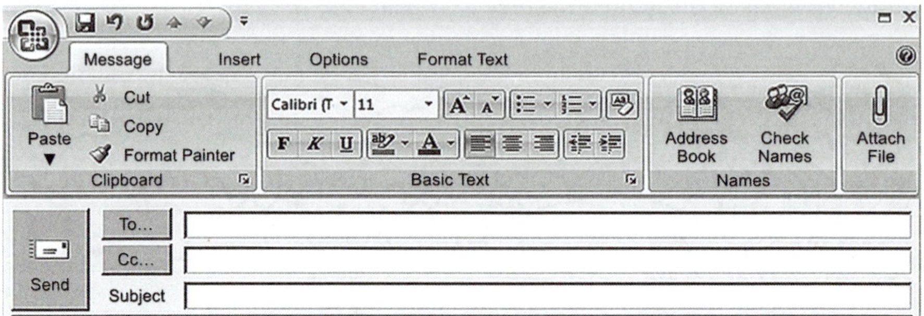


Dear Philipp,

How are ____________ ? My ____________ is Tom Shaw.

____________ in Eastbourne. It is a ____________

in England. I would like to ____________ more about

you and the town you live in. ____________ live in a

____________ town or in a ____________ village?

Do you have special sights in your town or village?

Where do you ____________ shopping?

Please ____________ back soon.

Take care

Tom

# Topic 11: In the countryside

Catherine's grandparents live in a village near Eastbourne. Catherine often visits them on Saturday or Sunday. They have got a big house with a beautiful garden and a barn for their animals.
On the farm live twelve hens, a cockerel, three pigs, two cats, a dog and a horse. The horse's name is Sammy.

In spring Catherine helps her grandmother in the garden. She loves the big trees and grandma's beautiful flowers. Catherine often works in grandpa's barn too. She feeds the animals and cleans the barn.

In summer, Catherine swims in the small lake next to the farm when it is hot. She often rides out with Sammy too. Then she is always very happy.

In autumn Catherine works in the garden again. Then she rakes the leaves and picks the apples off the trees.

In winter Catherine sits in their living room with her grandparents and they play card games. Sometimes it snows outside. She normally goes to bed early, because it is dark and she is so tired.

Catherine really loves her grandparents' farm.

**Fragen zum Text**

**72** Lies den Text gut durch und beantworte dann die Fragen in ganzen Sätzen.

a Where do Catherine's grandparents live?

______________________________

b What animals do Catherine's grandparents have?

______________________________

c Who is Sammy?

______________________________

d When does Catherine help her grandmother in the garden?

______________________________

e What does Catherine do in summer when it is hot?

______________________________

f When does Catherine rake the leaves?

______________________________

g Why does Catherine go to bed early in winter?

______________________________

**73** Lies dir den Text noch einmal durch. Kreuze an, ob die folgenden Aussagen richtig *(right)* oder falsch *(wrong)* sind.

| | | right | wrong |
|---|---|---|---|
| a | Catherine's grandparents have got a farm. | ☐ | ☐ |
| b | Their house is small. | ☐ | ☐ |
| c | They have got two pigs. | ☐ | ☐ |
| d | Catherine loves the garden because of the beautiful flowers. | ☐ | ☐ |
| e | Catherine never helps her grandfather. | ☐ | ☐ |
| f | Sometimes Catherine rides on a horse in summer. | ☐ | ☐ |
| g | Catherine never visits her grandparents in winter. | ☐ | ☐ |

## Grammatik

**Wann verwendest du den *s*-Genitiv?**

Der *s*-Genitiv zeigt an, **wem etwas gehört** oder **wer/was zu jemandem gehört**.
Er wird bei **Personen** und oft auch bei **Tieren** verwendet.

*Beispiele:* This is Lisa's bike. *Das ist Lisas Fahrrad.*
This is the dog's ball. *Das ist der Ball des Hundes.*

**Wie bildest du den *s*-Genitiv?**

Du bildest den ***s*-Genitiv im Singular** (Einzahl), indem du an die Singular-Form einen **Apostroph** (') und *s* anhängst.

*Beispiel:* Sarah's mobile phone

**74** Setze die richtige Form des *s*-Genitivs ein.

a ____________ car is pink. (Mrs Shaw)

b ____________ computer is new. (Tom)

c ____________ friends are nice. (Catherine)

d ____________ guitar is cool. (Trevor)

e London is ____________ capital. (England)

**75** Catherine stellt den Bauernhof ihrer Großeltern vor. Vervollständige die Sätze mithilfe der Angaben und der Bilder. Verwende den s-Genitiv.

a This is ____________.
(Grandma)

b This is the ____________.
(dog)

c This is the ______________________________.
(farm)

d This is ______________________________
______________________________.
(Grandma and Grandpa)

**Wortschatz**

**Wie heißen die verschiedenen Wochentage?**

| | | | |
|---|---|---|---|
| Monday | *Montag* | Friday | *Freitag* |
| Tuesday | *Dienstag* | Saturday | *Samstag* |
| Wednesday | *Mittwoch* | Sunday | *Sonntag* |
| Thursday | *Donnerstag* | | |

**76** Welcher Wochentag ist hier jeweils beschrieben?

a On this day there is no school. The next day is Monday.
It's ______________________________.

b The day after Tuesday is ______________________________.

c The day before Saturday is ______________________________.

d It is the fourth day of the week.
It's ______________________________.

e It is the second day of the week.
It's ______________________________.

f It is the first day of the week.
It's ______________________________.

g It is the first day of the weekend.
It's ______________________________.

**77** Welche Monate werden hier beschrieben? Schreibe den Namen des jeweiligen Monats in den äußeren Rand des Jahreskreises.

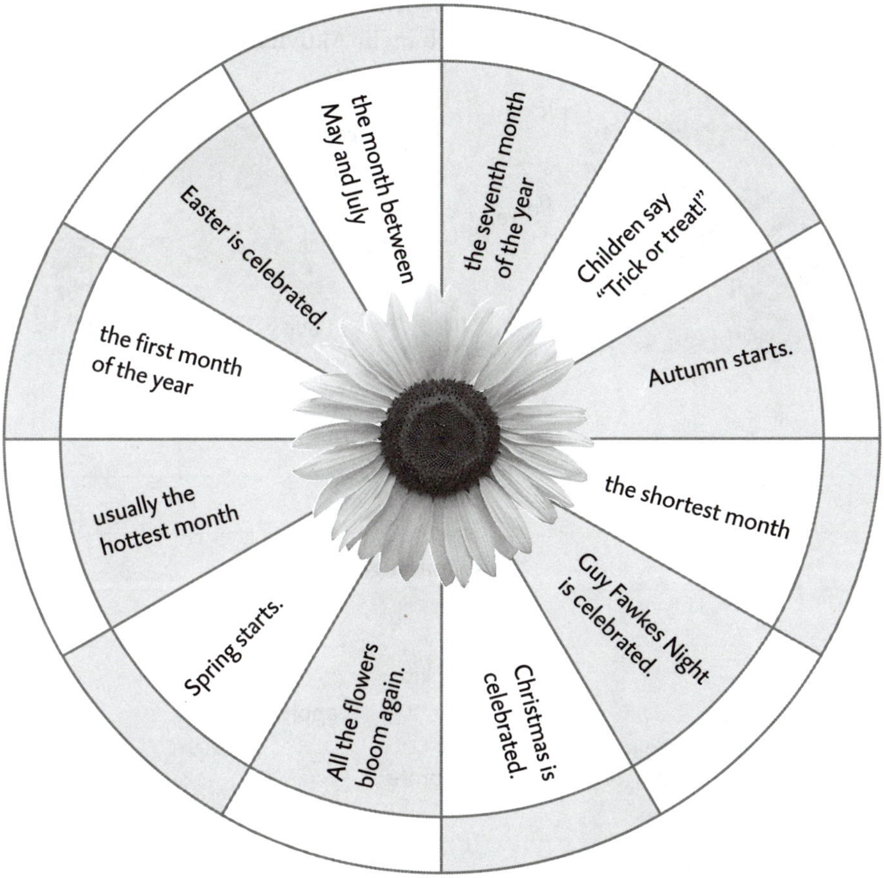

## Schreiben

**78** Was kann man zu verschiedenen Jahreszeiten machen? Bilde aus den Einzelwörtern Sätze und schreibe sie jeweils neben das richtige Bild. Wie heißen die Jahreszeiten auf Englisch? Fallen dir noch mehr Aktivitäten ein?

pick
Easter eggs
flowers
fly
ice cream
go
build
swimming
a kite
look for
apples
celebrate
eat
a snowman
on holiday
Christmas

# Topic 12: The London Eye

Tom's class is on a school trip to London. It is the capital of England and a very interesting city. The class walks through the city on the first day. They want to go to the "London Eye". It is a very big Ferris wheel in the centre of the city.

Tom and his classmates want to have a beautiful view of the city. But the London Eye is expensive. A single flight is £ 9.50 for a child and £ 17.95 for a person older than 15.

At the top of the Ferris wheel they can see a lot of famous London sights.

TOM: Look here on the left! That's the Houses of Parliament.
TREVOR: Yes, you are right. And that's Trafalgar Square over there.
TOM: Down here, you can see a lot of boats on the River Thames. Look, that's a big boat for a lot of people.
TREVOR: But look over there. That's Buckingham Palace. It's the home of Queen Elizabeth II. She lives and works there.
TOM: Oh, yes, let's go there next. Let's ask our teachers.

## Fragen zum Text

**79** Lies den Text genau durch. Kreuze die richtige Antwort an oder schreibe die richtige Antwort auf.

**a** Tom's class is on a ________________ to London.

**b** They want to go to …

- ☐ the Tower of London.
- ☐ the London Eye.
- ☐ the London Wheel.

**c** What is the London Eye?

______________________________________________

**d** How much is a single flight for a child?

£ __________

**e** What can Tom and Trevor see from the top of the Ferris wheel?

______________________________________________

______________________________________________

______________________________________________

______________________________________________

______________________________________________

______________________________________________

______________________________________________

**f** Next Tom wants to go …

- ☐ to the Houses of Parliament.
- ☐ to Trafalgar Square.
- ☐ to Buckingham Palace.

**g** It's the home of …

- ☐ Queen Elizabeth I.
- ☐ Queen Elizabeth II.
- ☐ the British Prime Minister.

**80** In den folgenden Sätzen stimmen die Adjektive nicht. Lies den Text noch einmal durch und schreibe den Satz noch einmal mit den richtigen Adjektiven auf.

**a** London is a very *boring* city.

___

**b** The class walks through the city on the *last* day of the school trip.

___

**c** The "London Eye" is a very *small* Ferris wheel.

___

**d** Tom and his classmates want to have a *rich* view of the city.

___

**e** A flight on the "London Eye" is *cheap*.

___

**f** At the top of the Ferris wheel they can see a lot of *old* London sights.

___

**g** Tom sees a *small* boat on the river.

___

## Grammatik

**Wann verwendest du *this* und wann *that*?**

- ***This*** verwendest du für eine **Person** oder **Sache** in der **Nähe** des Sprechers.
  *Beispiel:* This is a boy. *Dies ist ein Junge.*
- ***That*** verwendest du für eine **Person** oder **Sache** in einiger **Entfernung** vom Sprecher. Als **Signalwort** steht oft ***over there***.
  *Beispiel:* That is a girl over there. *(Das) dort drüben ist ein Mädchen.*

**In welcher Reihenfolge verwendest du *this* und *that*?**

Willst du zwei Personen oder Sachen **einander gegenüberstellen**, verwendest du zuerst *this* und dann *that*.

*Beispiele:* This is a car and that is a bike.
This is Mr Smith and that is Mrs Smith.

**81** Tom und seine Klasse sind auf dem Trafalgar Square. Vervollständige die Sätze jeweils mit *this* oder *that*. Sieh dir die Bilder genau an. Was befindet sich im Vordergrund des Bildes und was befindet sich im Hintergrund?

_____________ is the National Gallery.

_____________ is a lion.

_____________ is the church St Martin-in-the-Fields.

_____________ is a fountain.

_____________ is Big Ben.

_____________ is Nelson's Column.

**Wann verwendest du *these* und wann *those*?**

*These* und *those* sind die **Pluralformen** (Mehrzahlformen) von *this* und *that*. ***These*** verwendest du also für Personen und Dinge in der **Nähe** des Sprechers und ***those*** für Personen und Dinge in einiger **Entfernung** vom Sprecher.

*Beispiele:* These are cars and those are bikes over there.

**82** Hier siehst du eine Straße in London. Vervollständige die Sätze jeweils mit *these* oder *those*.

## Wortschatz

**83** Welche Sehenswürdigkeiten in London kennst du bereits? Beschrifte folgende Bilder.

## Schreiben

**84** Beschreibe das Bild. So kannst du anfangen:

On the left I can see ______________________________

______________________________

On the right ______________________________

______________________________

In the back ______________________________

______________________________

In the front ______________________________

______________________________

In the middle ______________________________

______________________________

**85** Schreibe eine kurze E-Mail an einen englischen Freund/eine englische Freundin und erzähle ihm/ihr, welche Londoner Sehenswürdigkeiten du gerne besuchen würdest und warum.
Hier sind ein paar Ideen: Buckingham Palace *(see the Queen?)*, London Zoo *(interesting animals)*, Madame Tussauds *(famous people)*, Hamley's in Regent Street *(toys)*, the Tower of London *(crown jewels)*

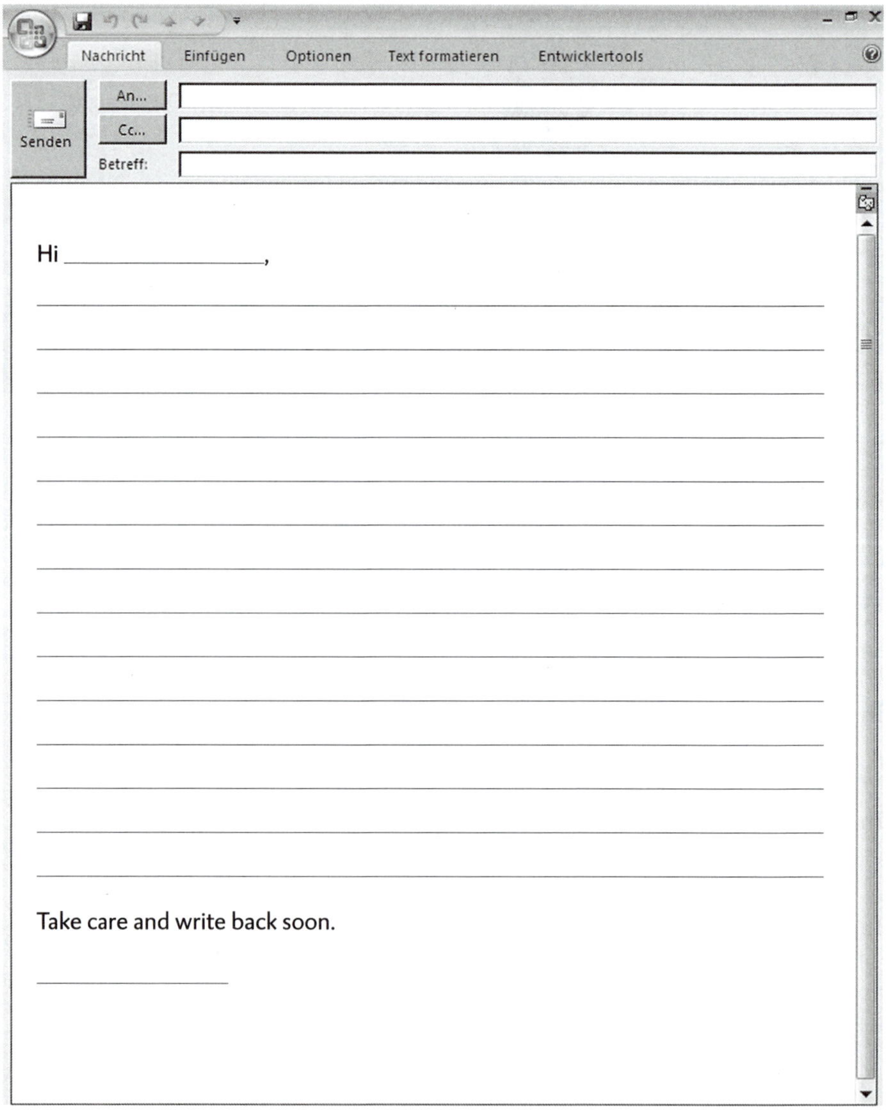

## Topic 13: Tom's dream

Tom is still in London with his class. Today they will visit Twickenham Rugby Stadium.
It is the stadium where the English national team plays all its games.
Tom loves rugby. He would like to become a rugby star.

The stadium is really big because it is a stadium for 82 000 people. Tom's class will do the stadium tour. They will see where the Queen sits during a match. They will also see where the players change their clothes and where they sit during the match when they are not playing. But Tom is sad that they won't see a match.

TREVOR: Will you buy an English team rugby shirt, Tom?
TOM: Of course I will! It is white with a red rose on it.

After the tour Tom and Trevor go to the fan shop:

TREVOR: Tom, look, there is a poster of Jonny Wilkinson! Your favourite star!
TOM: Yes, that's right. One day I'll play in this stadium for our national rugby team like him!
TREVOR: Oh, Tom. Do you really believe that?
TOM: Yes, I do. That's my dream!

### Fragen zum Text

**86** Lies dir den Text gut durch. Überprüfe die nachfolgenden Aussagen daraufhin, ob sie richtig *(right)* oder falsch *(wrong)* sind.

| | | right | wrong |
|---|---|---|---|
| **a** | Tom's class will visit Twickenham Football Stadium. | ☐ | ☐ |
| **b** | It's not a very big stadium. | ☐ | ☐ |
| **c** | They will see a match there. | ☐ | ☐ |
| **d** | Tom wants to buy a rugby shirt. | ☐ | ☐ |
| **e** | Jonny Wilkinson is a famous rugby player. | ☐ | ☐ |
| **f** | Tom is a big fan of Jonny Wilkinson. | ☐ | ☐ |
| **g** | Tom doesn't want to be a rugby player. | ☐ | ☐ |

**87** Lies den Text noch einmal durch und kreuze die richtige Antwort an.

**a** Twickenham Stadium is a stadium for …

☐ 8 200 people.

☐ 82 000 people.

☐ 820 000 people.

**b** During the stadium tour you can see …

☐ where the Queen sits.

☐ where the reporters sit.

☐ where the cameras are.

**c** What does the English team rugby shirt look like?

☐

☐

☐

**d** In the fan shop Trevor sees …

- ☐ a picture of the Queen.
- ☐ Jonny Wilkinson's rugby shirt.
- ☐ a poster of Jonny Wilkinson.

## Grammatik

**Wann verwendest du das *will-future* (Zukunftsform mit *will*)?**

- Du verwendest das *will-future*, wenn du **Vermutungen oder Vorhersagen** darüber anstellen willst, was in der Zukunft geschehen wird.
  *Beispiel:* It will be a great holiday. *Es wird ein toller Urlaub werden.*
- Häufig wird es nach Ausdrücken wie *think* oder *hope* oder *be sure* verwendet.
  *Beispiele:* I hope the sun will shine tomorrow.
  We think they will go to New York.
  He's sure you will pass the test.

**Wie bildest du das *will-future*?**

- Du bildest das *will-future* mit ***will* + Grundform des Verbs**. *Will* ist für alle Personen gleich.
  *Beispiel:* Mary will be happy. *Kurzform:* Mary'll be happy
- Die **verneinte** Form von *will* lautet ***will not***.
  *Beispiel:* They will not go to the cinema. *Kurzform:* They won't go to the cinema.

**88** Setze jeweils die richtige Form des *will-future* ein.

**a** I'm sure we ______________ (visit) Twickenham Rugby Stadium tomorrow.

**b** Tom and Trevor ____________________ (have fun) in the stadium.

**c** Trevor _______________ (go) with Tom to the fan shop.

**d** The class ___________________ (not see) the Queen in the stadium.

**e** Jonny Wilkinson ________________ (not play) in the match today.

**f** Tom _______________ (buy) a rugby shirt.

**g** Tom hopes he _______________ (play) in this stadium one day.

**h** Trevor thinks Tom _____________________ (not be) a rugby star.

**Wie kannst du Fragen und Kurzantworten im *will-future* bilden?**

Bei Fragen steht *will* am Anfang des Satzes:

*Beispiel:* You <u>will</u> help me. → <u>Will</u> you help me?

*Du wirst mir helfen.* *Wirst du mir helfen?*

Möchtest du eine **Kurzantwort** geben, musst du Folgendes beachten:

- Antwortest du mit ***yes***, verwendest du die Langform ***will***.
  *Beispiel:* Will you go on holiday? Yes, <u>I will</u>.
- Antwortest du mit ***no***, verwendest du normalerweise ***won't***.
  *Beispiel:* Will you eat pizza? No, <u>I won't</u>.

**89** Bevor Catherine mit ihrer Klasse nach London fährt, stellen ihre Brüder ihr wieder viele Fragen. Setze die richtige Frage oder Kurzantwort im *will-future* ein.

**a** ______________________ go to London soon, Cathy? – Yes, I will.

**b** __________________ rain in London? – No, it won't.

**c** Will you be at home next Saturday? – Yes, ______________.

**d** ____________________ ride on the London Eye? – Yes, I will.

**e** ____________________ see a rugby match? – No, we won't.

**f** Will you visit the Queen? – No, ________________.

**g** Will she be in London? – No, ____________________.

**h** Will you buy us a souvenir? – Yes, __________________.

## Wortschatz

**90** Wer ist die berühmte Person, die hier beschrieben wird? Setze die richtigen Wörter in das Kreuzworträtsel ein. Füge dann die Buchstaben 9 bis 18 in das Lösungswort ein. Das Lösungswort ergibt schließlich die gesuchte Person.

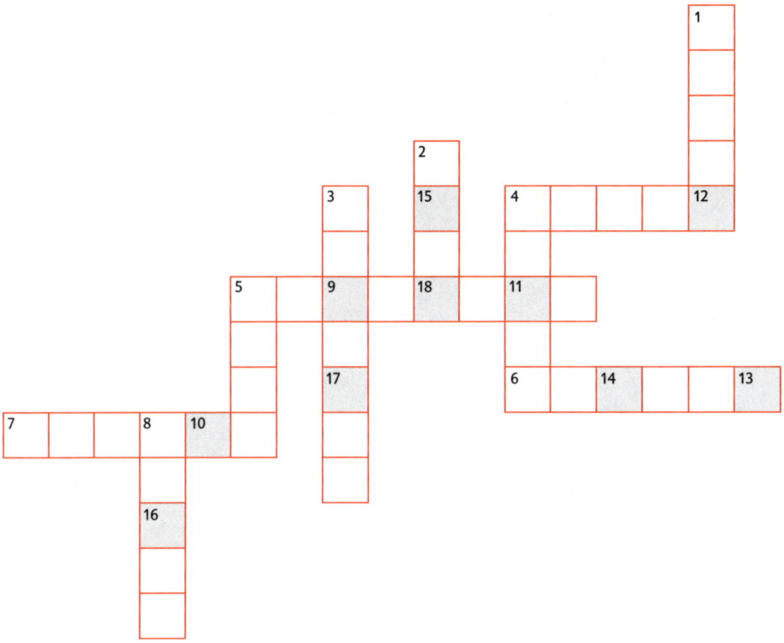

**Across →**

4 Sometimes she wears a beautiful ______________ on her head.
5 She has three sons and one ________________.
6 She doesn't live in a small house, she lives in a big ___________.
7 Her hobby is riding _______________.

**Down ↓**

1 The person we are looking for is not a man, she is a ____________.
2 She is not poor, she is ______________.
3 Great Britain is the name of the _______________ she lives in.
4 She doesn't wear ___________ clothes, she wears expensive clothes.
5 She often takes her _____________ for a walk.
8 You need to put this on a letter. You can see her head on it.

Her name is: Q __ __ __ __   __ __ __ Z __ B E __ __ II

(9 10 11 12   13 14 15   16   17 18)

**Schreiben**

**91** Jonny Wilkinson ist Toms Lieblingsstar. Wer ist dein Star? Fülle den folgenden Steckbrief aus.

# My star

name: ______________________

birthday: ______________________

job: ______________________

What do you know about him/her?

______________________________________

______________________________________

______________________________________

Why do you like him/her?

______________________________________

______________________________________

______________________________________

# Topic 14: A sightseeing tour

Today Tom and his class are going on a sightseeing tour through London. Tom is sitting in the front of the bus. His friend Trevor is sitting next to him. Susan and Vicky are sitting behind the two boys. The two girls are eating chocolate.

SUSAN: Tom and Trevor, would you like to have some chocolate?
TREVOR: Yes, thank you. Tom doesn't want to have chocolate. He is eating a sandwich.
TOM: I'm not eating a sandwich. I am eating a banana. But thank you.

*The bus is going through the city.*

VICKY: Look, here is Madame Tussauds. Oh dear, there are a lot of people in front of the entrance. Do they all want to visit the museum?
TREVOR: I think so. Everyone loves the waxwork museum. We're lucky that we are not visiting Madame Tussauds now. But look, that is Regent's Park, Tom. Some boys are playing rugby. They are really good!

*Now the bus is passing Buckingham Palace.*

TREVOR: Here lives our Queen! She is looking out of the window and is waving at us!
TOM: Let me see, Trevor, where is she? I can't see her!
TREVOR: I'm just joking. She isn't looking out of the window.
TOM AND SUSAN: Trevor!

### Fragen zum Text

**92** Lies dir den Text gut durch. Vervollständige dann die folgenden Sätze.

**a** Tom and his class are going on a ______________ ______________ through London.

**b** Tom is sitting next to ______________.

**c** There are ______________ in front of Madame Tussauds.

**d** Madame Tussauds is a ______________ ______________.

**e** Some ______________ are playing rugby in Regent's Park.

**f** The Queen ______________ in Buckingham Palace.

**g** ______________ can't see the Queen.

**93** Lies dir den Text noch einmal durch. Überprüfe die folgenden Aussagen darauf, ob sie richtig *(right)* oder falsch *(wrong)* sind. Schreibe den Satz richtig auf, falls die Aussage falsch ist.

| | right | wrong |
|---|---|---|
| **a** Tom is sitting in the back of the bus. | ☐ | ☐ |
| ______________________________ | | |
| **b** Tom is eating a sandwich. | ☐ | ☐ |
| ______________________________ | | |
| **c** A lot of people want to visit the waxwork museum. | ☐ | ☐ |
| ______________________________ | | |
| **d** The Queen is looking out of the window. | ☐ | ☐ |
| ______________________________ | | |
| **e** The bus is passing Hyde Park. | ☐ | ☐ |
| ______________________________ | | |
| **f** The bus is passing Buckingham Palace. | ☐ | ☐ |
| ______________________________ | | |

## Grammatik

**Wann verwendest du das *present progressive*?**

Du benutzt das ***present progressive*** (Verlaufsform der Gegenwart), um auszudrücken, was zum Zeitpunkt des Sprechens **gerade geschieht**. Im Deutschen drückst du dies zum Beispiel mit dem Wort „gerade" aus.

| | | |
|---|---|---|
| *Beispiele:* | He is cooking. | *Er kocht gerade.* |
| | They are cooking. | *Sie kochen gerade.* |

**Signalwörter** für das *present progressive* sind z. B.: *at the moment, (right) now*

**Wie bildest du das *present progressive*?**

- Du bildest das *present progressive*, indem du nach das Subjekt (Satzgegenstand) die folgenden Formen stellst: **Form von *be* + Verb in der *-ing*-Form**

| | |
|---|---|
| I am watching TV. | *Ich sehe fern.* |
| You are watching TV. | *Du siehst fern. / Sie sehen fern. (Höflichkeitsform)* |
| He/She/It is watching TV. | *Er/Sie/Es sieht fern.* |
| We are watching TV. | *Wir sehen fern.* |
| You are watching TV. | *Ihr seht fern. / Sie sehen fern. (Höflichkeitsform)* |
| They are watching TV. | *Sie sehen fern.* |

- In der Umgangssprache werden auch die **Kurzformen** verwendet:

*Beispiele:* I'm watching TV.
He's watching TV.
You're watching TV.

**94** Setze die richtige Form des *present progressive* ein.

It is 8 o'clock in the morning. Tom's class is having breakfast at a youth hostel in London.

a Tom ________________ (is/are – eat) cornflakes.

b Susan and Vicky ________________ (is/are – drink) milk.

c Trevor ________________ (is/are – laugh).

d The hostel's cat ________________ (is/are – play) with an apple.

e The teachers ________________ (is/are – talk) to some pupils.

f It ________________ (is/are – rain) outside.

g The bus driver ________________ (is/are – wait) for the pupils.

**Wie bildest du die Verneinung im *present progressive*?**
**Verneinte Sätze**, in denen das ***present progressive*** verwendet wird, bildest du folgendermaßen: **Form von *be* + *not* + Verb in der *ing*-Form**

| | | | |
|---|---|---|---|
| *Beispiele:* | I am not reading. | (*Kurzform:* I'm not reading.) | *Ich lese gerade nicht.* |
| | He is not reading. | (*Kurzform:* He isn't reading.) | *Er liest gerade nicht.* |
| | We are not reading. | (*Kurzform:* We aren't reading.) | *Wir lesen gerade nicht.* |

Wenn du diese Form benutzt, kannst du sagen, was gerade **nicht** passiert.

**95** Setze bei den folgenden Sätzen die richtige Form des *present progressive* ein.

It is one o'clock in the afternoon. What are the pupils doing or not doing in London at the moment?

**a** The pupils are ______________________ (not go) to a restaurant.
They ______________________ (go) to a park.

**b** Susan ______________________ (not listen) to Trevor's jokes.
She ______________________ (listen) to music.

**c** Vicky ______________________ (not take) a photo of the Queen.
She ______________________ (take) a photo of Tom.

**d** Tom ______________________ (not buy) a silly hat for his father.
He ______________________ (buy) a silly hat for his sister Becky.

**e** The pupils ______________________ (not wait) for a taxi.
They ______________________ (wait) for the bus.

**Wie bildest du Fragen im *present progressive*?**

**Fragesätze** im ***present progressive*** bildest du, indem du die jeweils richtige Form von *be* an den Satzanfang stellst:

| | | | |
|---|---|---|---|
| *Beispiele:* | You are reading. | Are you reading? | *Liest du gerade?* |
| | He is reading. | Is he reading? | *Liest er gerade?* |

**96** Bringe die folgenden Fragesätze in die richtige Reihenfolge.

It is now 3 o'clock in the afternoon. The class is in Regent's Park. Susan and Vicky are sitting in the grass. Susan is asking some questions.

**a** is – a map of London – Tom – looking at?

______________________________

**b** a photo – taking – of Tom – Trevor – is?

______________________________

**c** playing – rugby – are – the boys?

______________________________

**d** playing – the dog – is – with the ball?

______________________________

**e** Trevor – is – telling – jokes?

______________________________

**f** we now – are – back to the youth hostel – going?

______________________________

**Wortschatz**

**97** Wo kann man die folgenden Dinge in London kaufen oder essen? Ordne die Gegenstände dem jeweiligen Ort zu und vervollständige dann die Sätze mit den passenden Wörtern.

1. You can buy a ________________ in a post office.
2. You can eat ____________________ in a pub.
3. You can buy a _________________ in Camden ________________.
4. You can buy a _______________________ for the London tube at an _______________________ station.
5. You can buy ____________________ at a souvenir _____________________.

## Schreiben

**98** Beschreibe, was auf dem Bild gerade geschieht. Vervollständige die Sätze und verwende dabei das *present progressive*. Benutze die folgenden Verben:
*stand – walk – cross – wait*

______________________ the street.

People ______________________ on the pavement *(Gehweg)*.

A man is ______________________ .

People ______________________ to cross the street.

# Topic 15: Mind the gap!

Here are some rules and tips for your visit to London:

You must look right before you cross the street!

You must mind the gap[1] when you enter a train in the London Underground.

Don't forget an umbrella because it often rains in London.

Don't forget a map! London is a very big city.

You need British pounds to pay in London but you can change your money.

You must see the Changing of the Guard at Buckingham Palace at 11.30 a.m.

You must visit the Natural History Museum because you can see dinosaurs there.

You must visit Harrod's. It is a very big department store.

You must visit Madame Tussauds because you can see all the famous stars in wax there.

You must write postcards to your best friends before you leave London.

1 to mind sth.: *auf etw. aufpassen*; gap: *Spalt, Lücke*

**Fragen zum Text**

**99** Lies dir den Text gut durch. In die folgenden Ratschläge haben sich Fehler eingeschlichen. Verbessere sie mithilfe des Textes.

a You must look left before you cross a street in London!

_______________

b Don't mind the gap when you enter the London Underground.

_______________

c Don't buy a map.

_______________

d You can pay with Euro in London.

_______________

e Don't visit the Natural History Museum.

_______________

f You must visit Harrods, a very big museum.

_______________

**100** Lies den Text noch einmal. Beantworte dann die Fragen mit 1 bis 5 Wörtern.

a What do you often need in London because it rains a lot?

_______________

b When is the Changing of the Guard?

_______________

c What can you see at the Natural History Museum?

_______________

d Who can you see at Madame Tussauds?

_______________

e What must you do before you leave London?

_______________

## Grammatik

**Welche Formen von *can* und *must* gibt es?**

*Can* (können) und *must* (müssen) haben **bei allen Personen die gleiche Form.**

| | | | |
|---|---|---|---|
| *1. Person Singular* | I can/must | *1. Person Plural* | we can/must |
| *2. Person Singular* | you can/must | *2. Person Plural* | you can/must |
| *3. Person Singular* | he, she, it can/must | *3. Person Plural* | they can/must |

**Wann verwendest du *can*?**

Du benutzt ***can***, wenn du ausdrücken willst, dass etwas **möglich** ist oder dass jemand die **Fähigkeit** besitzt, etwas Bestimmtes zu tun.
Bei der **Verneinung** wird im gesprochenen und geschriebenen Englisch häufig die Kurzform ***can't*** verwendet, die Langform ist *cannot*.

| Aussagesatz | verneinter Satz | Fragesatz |
|---|---|---|
| He can swim. | I can't/cannot swim | Can I eat the cake? |
| *Er kann schwimmen.* | *Ich kann nicht schwimmen.* | *Darf/Kann ich den Kuchen essen?* |

**101** Bilde mit den folgenden Satzteilen fünf Sätze mit *can* oder *can't*.

| | | |
|---|---|---|
| I | can | speak German. |
| Trevor | can't /cannot | play the piano. |
| Tom and Catherine | Can you … | help me. |
| | Can I … | help me? |
| | | help you. |

_______________________________________________

_______________________________________________

_______________________________________________

_______________________________________________

_______________________________________________

**Wann verwendest du *must*?**

***Must*** wird benutzt, wenn etwas **notwendig** ist.

*Beispiel:* I <u>must wash</u> my hands. *Ich muss meine Hände waschen.*

**102** Setze die richtige Form ein: *can/can't* oder *must.*

**a** In Germany, you ____________ be 17 years old to drive a car.

**b** You ____________ be careful when you cross the road in England because the cars come from the right.

**c** You ____________ visit Buckingham Palace today because it isn't open.

**d** Jenny ____________ play the guitar, but she can't play the piano.

### Wortschatz

**103** Was kann man an einem Tag in London machen? Fülle die Lücken mit den folgenden Verben:

| see – take – listen – walk – visit – watch – ride – speak |
| --- |

a You can ____________________ the London Underground.

b You can ____________________ a museum.

c You can ____________________ the Changing of the Guard.

d You can ____________________ on a red London bus.

e You can ____________________ the Queen at Madame Tussauds.

f You can ____________________ to Big Ben, the clock.

g You can ____________________ through London Zoo.

h You can ____________________ English in London!

### Schreiben

**104** Welche Tipps würdest du Tom für den Ort, in dem du lebst, geben? Was muss er unbedingt sehen und tun? Du kannst die Wörter im Kasten verwenden.

| must can can't look left first visit see pay be careful because |
| --- |

In my town you … ____________________________________________

____________________________________________

____________________________________________

____________________________________________

____________________________________________

____________________________________________

____________________________________________

## Topic 16: Zoe's birthday party

Today is Zoe's birthday. She is now eleven years old and it is the day of her party with her friends. But first she goes to the shop in her street because she needs some more things for the party.

SHOP ASSISTANT: Hello Zoe, can I help you?
ZOE: Yes, I'd like to have five bottles of lemonade, please.
SHOP ASSISTANT: Here you are.
ZOE: How much is it?
SHOP ASSISTANT: It's £ 3.99. Would you like anything else?
ZOE: Yes, three packets of crisps and two boxes of ice cream, please.
SHOP ASSISTANT: Here you are. Anything else?
ZOE: No, thank you. How much is it now?
SHOP ASSISTANT: It's £ 11.49.
ZOE: Here you are. Thank you, bye.
SHOP ASSISTANT: Bye, have a nice day, Zoe.

Back home all her friends are already in front of the house.

TOM: Happy birthday, Zoe! Look, here are our presents for you.
ZOE: So many presents! Thank you so much! Please come inside. Let's have something to drink and eat now.

### Fragen zum Text

**105** Lies den Text genau durch und kreuze jeweils die richtige Antwort an.

**a** Zoe is now …
- ☐ 11 years old.
- ☐ 10 years old.
- ☐ 12 years old.

**b** At the shop she buys things for …
- ☐ her mother's birthday party.
- ☐ her birthday party.
- ☐ her friend's birthday party.

**c** Zoe goes to the shop because …
- ☐ she needs some more presents.
- ☐ she needs some more things for her birthday party.
- ☐ she has to buy something for her mother.

**d** Zoe buys …
- ☐ five bottles of lemonade, four packets of crisps and two boxes of ice cream.
- ☐ five bottles of lemonade, three packets of crisps and four boxes of ice cream.
- ☐ five bottles of lemonade, three packets of crisps and two boxes of ice cream.

**e** She has to pay …
- ☐ £ 11.49.
- ☐ £ 111.49.
- ☐ £ 3.49.

**f** Zoe's friends are already …
- ☐ in front of her house.
- ☐ in front of the shop.
- ☐ inside her house.

**g** Zoe's friends have …
- ☐ a big present for her.
- ☐ a lot of presents for her.
- ☐ no present for her.

**106** In die folgenden Sätze aus dem Text haben sich Fehler eingeschlichen. Lies den Text noch einmal durch und schreibe die Sätze richtig auf.

a The shop is far away.

______________________________

b Five bottles of lemonade cost £ 3.89.

______________________________

c Zoe also buys some chocolate.

______________________________

______________________________

d Zoe has to pay twelve pounds and forty-four pence.

______________________________

______________________________

### Grammatik

**Wann verwendest du *many* und wann verwendest du *much*?**

Manchmal willst du die genaue Zahl nicht sagen. Im Deutschen kannst du „viele“ oder „viel“ sagen. Auf Englisch bedeutet „viele“ = *many* und „viel“ = *much*.

- Du verwendest *many* für **zählbare** Dinge.
  Diese gezählten Gegenstände stehen im Plural (Mehrzahl).
  *Beispiel:* How many presents are in the photo?

- Du verwendest *much* für etwas, das **nicht gezählt werden kann** und wo du z. B. nicht zwei ..., drei ... usw. sagen kannst. Diese Wörter haben keine Pluralform.
  *Beispiel:* How much butter do you need for the cake?

**107** Vervollständige die folgenden Sätze mithilfe der Bilder. Entscheide, ob du *many* oder *much* verwenden musst.

**a** Mr Shaw hasn't got ____________________ shoes.

**b** This isn't ______________________________.

**c** There are so ________________________________________.

**d** Don't eat so ________________________________________!

**e** Tom doesn't drink

__________________________________.

**Nützliche Wendungen für den Einkauf**

| | |
|---|---|
| How much is it? | *Wie viel kostet es?* |
| Anything else? | *Darf es noch etwas sein?* |
| What would you like? | *Was möchten Sie/möchtest du?* |
| I would like .../ I'd like ... | *Ich hätte gerne .../ Ich würde gerne ...* |

**108** Lies dir die nützlichen Wendungen für den Einkauf durch (siehe oben). Setze dann die richtigen Wendungen in den folgenden Dialog ein:

SHOP ASSISTANT: Hello, can I help you? What ____________________?

MARY: I ________________ to buy a dress. ________________ this dress?

SHOP ASSISTANT: This dress is £40.

MARY: Oh. That's too expensive for me. Have you got a cheaper dress?

SHOP ASSISTANT: Yes, I have. Look, these two dresses only cost £25.

MARY: Yes, I like those dresses! And the price is OK. I ______________ to try them on.

SHOP ASSISTANT: Do you need ________________?

MARY: No, thank you. That's enough for the moment.

## Wortschatz

**Wann verwendest du die Grundzahlen?**

Mit **Grundzahlen** gibst du eine **bestimmte Anzahl** und nicht eine bestimmte Reihenfolge an. Eine Grundzahl antwortet also auf die Frage **„wie viele?"**.

**Grundzahlen bis 100**

| | | | | | | | |
|---|---|---|---|---|---|---|---|
| 1 | one | 11 | eleven | 21 | twenty-one | 90 | ninety |
| 2 | two | 12 | twelve | 22 | twenty-two | 100 | one hundred (a hundred) |
| 3 | three | 13 | thirteen | 23 | twenty-three | | |
| 4 | four | 14 | fourteen | | usw. | | |
| 5 | five | 15 | fifteen | 30 | thirty | | |
| 6 | six | 16 | sixteen | 40 | forty | | |
| 7 | seven | 17 | seventeen | 50 | fifty | | |
| 8 | eight | 18 | eighteen | 60 | sixty | | |
| 9 | nine | 19 | nineteen | 70 | seventy | | |
| 10 | ten | 20 | twenty | 80 | eighty | | |

**109** Füge jeweils das Alter ein. Schreibe die Zahl aus.

I'm ______________________
(75) years old.

I'm ______________________
(3) years old.

I'm ______________________
(39) years old.

We are ______________________
(17) years old.

I'm ______________________
(200) years old.

**Wann verwendest du Ordnungszahlen?**

Mit **Ordnungszahlen** gibst du eine **bestimmte Reihenfolge** an. Eine Ordnungszahl antwortet also auf die Frage **„der / die wievielte?"**.

*Beispiel:* This is the third time you're late. *Du bist zum dritten Mal zu spät.*

**Die Ordnungszahlen bis 10:**

| | | | |
|---|---|---|---|
| 1st | first | 6th | sixth |
| 2nd | second | 7th | seventh |
| 3rd | third | 8th | eighth |
| 4th | fourth | 9th | ninth |
| 5th | fifth | 10th | tenth |

**Merke:** Im Deutschen steht nach der Ordnungszahl ein **Punkt**, im Englischen die **beiden letzten Buchstaben** der Ordnungszahl.

*Beispiel:* 2nd *(englische Schreibweise)* 2. *(deutsche Schreibweise)*

**110** Sieh dir das folgende Klingelschild an. In welchem Stockwerk wohnen die einzelnen Familien? Vervollständige die Sätze auf der nächsten Seite.

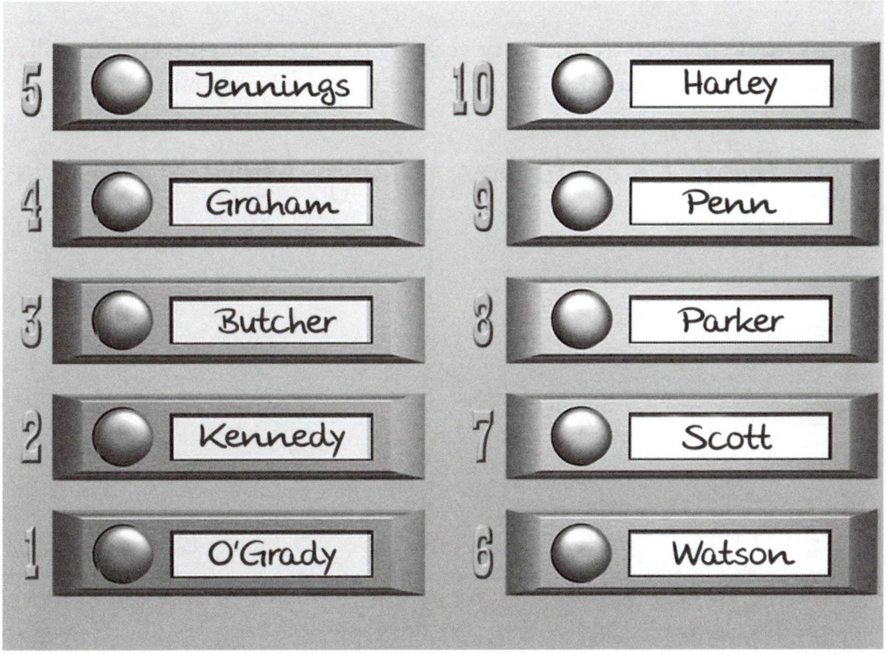

a The Watsons live *on the sixth (6th) floor* ______.

b The Kennedys live ______.

c The Grahams ______.

d The Penns ______.

e The Parkers ______.

f The O'Gradys ______.

g The Butchers ______.

h The Jennings ______.

i The Scotts ______.

j The Harleys ______.

**Schreiben**

**111** Du möchtest eine Geburtstagsparty veranstalten. Schreibe eine Liste mit allen Dingen, die du für deine Party brauchst, und was du alles noch machen musst.

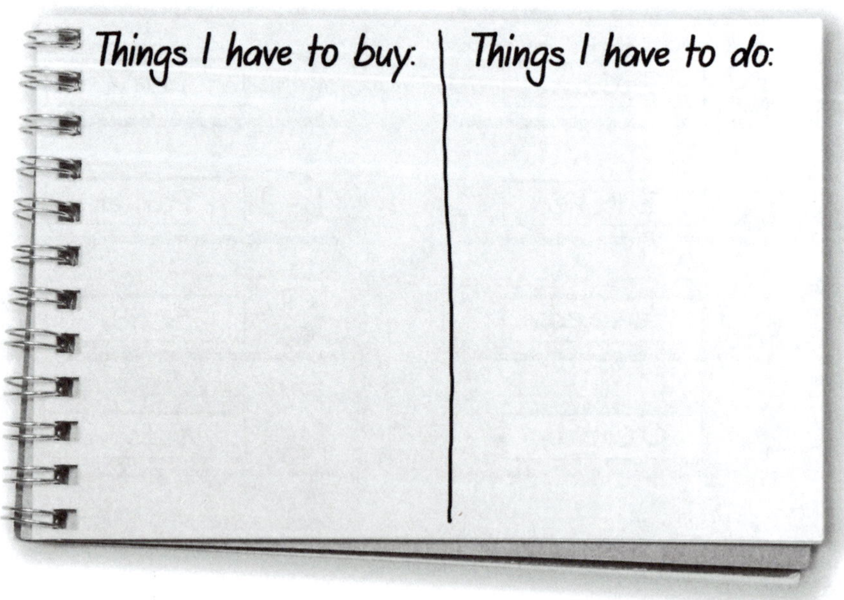

**112** Vervollständige folgende Einladungskarte für deine Geburtstagsparty.

Dear

_______________,

I would like to invite you to my

_________________________________.

It takes place on _____________ (*Wochentag*),

_________ (*Zahl*) ________________ (*Monat*).

It ______ at _______ in the afternoon. (*Uhrzeit*)

Please _______ me an e-mail or _____________

me to tell me if you can come.

See you!

Yours

____________________

(your name)

## Topic 17: Holiday activities

Catherine and Zoe want to go on holiday. Yesterday Catherine was at Zoe's house. They looked at a holiday brochure:

### Fernando's Sports Camp, Tarifa/Spain

Have fun in the sun and in the sea of southern Spain. Relax on the beach or do some water sports.

**Activities:** windsurfing, water skiing, scuba diving

**Cost per week: £ 400** **Age: from 11 to 18**

### Heinrich Müller Language School Cologne/Germany

Learn German in a German city.

Join our fast language learning programme and have fun in the attractive city of Cologne.

Don't forget to visit the famous cathedral of Cologne!

**Activities:** language learning, sightseeing tours, theatre group

**Cost per week:** £ 250 **Age:** from 10 to 16

### Madame Michelle's Arts Camp, Paris/France

Have fun in the romantic city of Paris and learn to paint like Pablo Picasso.

Visit the Louvre, the world famous art museum, climb the Eiffel Tower and enjoy the fantastic view of Paris.

**Activities:** painting, visiting museums, sightseeing

**Cost per week:** £ 200

**Age:** from 10 to 18

## Fragen zum Text

**113** Lies die Texte zu den einzelnen Feriencamps gut durch. Welche Angebote haben Catherine und Zoe gewählt? Was käme für Trevor und Tom infrage? Schreibe den Namen des Angebots in die Tabelle.

| | |
|---|---|
| **Catherine** likes animals, especially her horse, Jewel. She would like to have a painting of Jewel, but doesn't know how to paint. | |
| **Zoe** loves dancing. When she is older she wants to be a professional dancer and singer. | |
| **Trevor** would like to speak German better, because he wants to visit his German grandmother, who can't speak English. | |
| **Tom** likes playing rugby, but during the summer holidays he would like to try out a new sport. | |

**114** Lies den Text genau durch und kreuze die richtige Antwort an.

**a** Fernando's Sports Camp is for children …
- ☐ from 4 to 18.
- ☐ from 11 to 18.
- ☐ from 10 to 15.

**b** At the sports camp you can do …
- ☐ windsurfing.
- ☐ skiing.
- ☐ sightseeing.

**c** At the Heinrich Müller Language School you can learn …
- ☐ French.
- ☐ English.
- ☐ German.

**d** In Paris you can climb …
- ☐ the Eiffel Tower.
- ☐ Cologne Cathedral.
- ☐ the Louvre.

**e** The Louvre in Paris is …
- ☐ an art museum.
- ☐ a sports museum.
- ☐ a history museum.

**f** The Super Dance Academy is in …
- ☐ France.
- ☐ England.
- ☐ Germany.

**g** At the Super Dance Academy you can also take …
- ☐ swimming lessons.
- ☐ singing lessons.
- ☐ language courses.

## Grammatik

**Wie bildest du das *simple past*?**
Die Form des *simple past* ist **für alle Personen gleich**.
Normalerweise hängst du ***-ed*** an die Grundform des Verbs an.
*Beispiel:* watch → watched

**Wann verwendest du das *simple past*?**
Du verwendest das *simple past*, wenn du von in der **Vergangenheit abgeschlossenen Handlungen und Zuständen** berichten willst.
*Beispiel:* Last year I learned to ski. *Letztes Jahr lernte ich Skifahren.*

**115** Vervollständige die folgenden Sätze jeweils mit der *simple past*-Form oder der *simple present*-Form des Verbs in Klammern.

a This year I ________________ to ski.

Last year I ________________ to paint. (learn)

b Yesterday, Tom ________________ the latest Harry Potter film.

He often ________________ a film in the cinema. (watch)

c Every year a lot of tourists ________________ Paris.

Last month Catherine ________________ Paris, too. (visit)

d Usually I ________________ at home,

but yesterday I ________________ on the beach. (relax)

e Now I ________________ in Eastbourne.

Five years ago I ________________ in London. (live)

f Last week John ________________ football,

but he usually ________________ tennis. (play)

Viele englische Verben haben eine **unregelmäßige Form** im *past tense*, d. h., sie bilden die Vergangenheitsform nicht mit *-ed*.
Unregelmäßige Verbformen musst du auswendig lernen.
Beim Verb *be* gibt es zwei Formen. Bei allen anderen unregelmäßigen Verben sind die Formen für alle Personen gleich.

| | | | | |
|---|---|---|---|---|
| *Beispiele:* | be → | I was | go | → went |
| | | you were | make | → made |
| | | he/she/it was | do | → did |
| | | we were | say | → said |
| | | they were | | |

**116** Nach den Ferien erzählen Catherine, Zoe, Tom und Trevor von ihren Erlebnissen. Setze jeweils die richtige Form des *simple past* ein.

**a** TOM: I ______________ (go) to Fernando's Sports Camp.
It ______________ (be) fun!

**b** CATHERINE: I ______________ (do) painting at Madame Michelle's Arts Camp in Paris.
It ______________ (be) fantastic!

**c** ZOE: I ______________ (be) in Liverpool.
I ______________ (learn) to dance!

**d** TREVOR: I ______________ (make) a lot of new friends at the language school in Cologne.
Everyone ______________ (say) it ______________ (be) great!

**Wortschatz**

**117** Im Sand findest du verschiedene Wörter zum Thema „Summer holidays“. Vervollständige mit diesen Wörtern die Mindmap.

## Schreiben

**118** Catherine schreibt dir eine Postkarte von ihrem Ferienaufenthalt auf dem Bauernhof ihrer Großeltern. Schreibe ihr eine Postkarte aus deinem Urlaub.

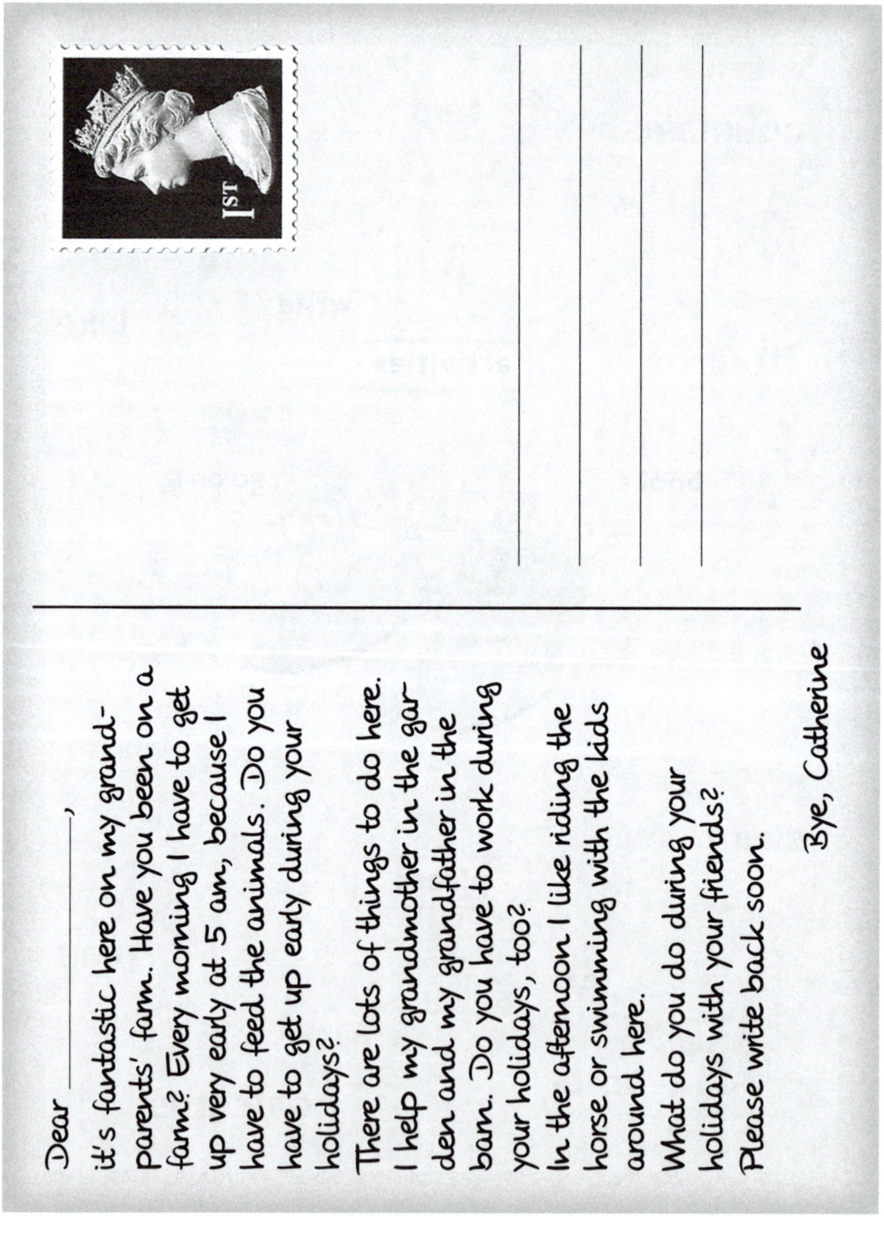

1ST

Dear ______________,
it's fantastic here on my grandparents' farm. Have you been on a farm? Every morning I have to get up very early at 5 am, because I have to feed the animals. Do you have to get up early during your holidays?
There are lots of things to do here. I help my grandmother in the garden and my grandfather in the barn. Do you have to work during your holidays, too?
In the afternoon I like riding the horse or swimming with the kids around here.
What do you do during your holidays with your friends? Please write back soon.
Bye, Catherine

Dear Catherine,

______________________________

______________________________

______________________________

______________________________

______________________________

______________________________

______________________________

______________________________

______________________________

______________________________

Bye, ________________

Catherine Smith
57 Brighton Road
Eastbourne BE21 1AB

Great Britain

# Vocabulary

Auf den folgenden Seiten kannst du Wörter aus dem Buch nachschlagen, die neu für dich sind oder die du vergessen hast. Markiere dir diese Vokabeln am besten in der Liste und im Text und wiederhole sie regelmäßig. Du kannst mit dieser Liste aber auch deinen Wortschatz erweitern. Decke z. B. eine Seite mit einem Blatt Papier zu und schreibe das englische Wort auf das Blatt. Nimm dir aber nicht zu viel auf einmal vor, etwa sieben neue Wörter pro Tag genügen. Du kannst die Wörter und Wendungen aber auch auf Karteikarten schreiben und in einem Vokabelkasten folgendermaßen sortieren: die Wörter, die du noch nicht beherrscht, kommen in das erste Fach. Diejenigen, die du schon gut kannst, in das zweite und Wörter, die du ganz sicher beherrscht, in das dritte Fach. Vergiss aber nicht, auch die Wörter im zweiten und dritten Fach regelmäßig zu wiederholen.

# Vocabulary

| | | |
|---|---|---|
| **Aa** | a/an | ein, eine |
| | a little bit | ein wenig, ein bisschen |
| | a lot of / lots of | viele |
| | about | ungefähr |
| | academy | Akademie |
| | activity | Aktion, Tätigkeit |
| | address | Adresse |
| | after | nach |
| | afternoon | Nachmittag |
| | again | wieder |
| | age | Alter |
| | all | alle, alles |
| | all over | überall |
| | along | entlang |
| | already | schon, bereits |
| | also | auch |
| | always | immer |
| | and | und |
| | angry | verärgert |
| | animal | Tier |
| | Anything else? | Darf es noch etwas sein? |
| | apple | Apfel |
| | April | April |
| | around | in der Nähe, ringsum |
| | (to) arrive | ankommen |
| | art | Kunst |
| | (to) ask | fragen |
| | at | an, auf, in |
| | at home | zu Hause |
| | at the moment | im Moment, gerade |
| | attractive | attraktiv |
| | August | August |
| | aunt | Tante |
| | away | weg |
| **Bb** | baby | Baby |
| | back | *hier:* Hintergrund |

| | |
|---|---|
| bacon | Schinken |
| bag | Tasche |
| baked beans | gebackene Bohnen |
| ball | Ball |
| banana | Banane |
| barn | Scheune, Stall |
| basket | Korb |
| basketball | Basketball |
| bathroom | Badezimmer |
| (to) be | sein |
| beach | Strand |
| beautiful | schön |
| because | weil |
| (to) become | werden |
| bed | Bett |
| bedroom | Schlafzimmer |
| before | bevor |
| behind | hinter |
| (to) believe | glauben |
| best | bester, beste, bestes |
| big | groß |
| bike | Fahrrad |
| biology | Biologie |
| birthday | Geburtstag |
| black | schwarz |
| blackboard | Tafel |
| (to) bloom | blühen |
| blue | blau |
| boat | Boot, Schiff |
| body | Körper |
| book | Buch |
| bookshelf | Bücherregal |
| boring | langweilig |
| both | beide, beides |
| bottle | Flasche |
| box | Box, Schachtel |
| boy | Junge |
| bread | Brot |
| break | Pause |

| | | |
|---|---|---|
| | breakfast | Frühstück |
| | brochure | Broschüre |
| | brother | Bruder |
| | brown | braun |
| | (to) build | bauen |
| | bus | Bus |
| | but | aber |
| | butter | Butter |
| | (to) buy | kaufen |
| | bye | Tschüss |
| **Cc** | cafeteria | Kantine, Cafeteria |
| | cake | Kuchen |
| | (to) call someone | jemanden (an)rufen |
| | camera | Kamera |
| | can | können |
| | capital | Hauptstadt |
| | car | Auto |
| | careful | vorsichtig |
| | (to) carry | tragen |
| | cat | Katze |
| | cathedral | Kathedrale |
| | CD-Player | CD-Spieler |
| | (to) celebrate | feiern |
| | centre | Zentrum, Mitte |
| | chair | Stuhl |
| | (to) change | wechseln |
| | Changing of the Guard | Wachwechsel (vor dem Buckingham Palace in London) |
| | cheap | billig |
| | cheese | Käse |
| | child, children | Kind, Kinder |
| | chips | Pommes frites |
| | chocolate | Schokolade |
| | choir | Chor |
| | church | Kirche |
| | cinema | Kino |
| | city | (große) Stadt |
| | class | (Schul)Klasse |

| | |
|---|---|
| class teacher | Klassenlehrer, Klassenlehrerin |
| classmate | Klassenkamerad, Klassenkameradin |
| classroom | Klassenraum |
| (to) clean | sauber machen, putzen |
| (to) climb | hinaufsteigen, hinaufklettern |
| clock | Uhr |
| clothes | Kleidung |
| cockerel | Hahn |
| coffee | Kaffee |
| coke | Cola |
| colour | Farbe |
| column | Säule |
| (to) come | kommen |
| comprehensive school | Gesamtschule |
| computer | Computer |
| (to) cook | kochen |
| cornflakes | Cornflakes |
| (to) cost | kosten |
| country | Land |
| (in the) countryside | (auf dem) Land |
| cousin | Cousin, Cousine |
| crab | Krabbe |
| cricket | Cricket (englisches Rasenspiel) |
| crisps | Kartoffelchips |
| (to) cross | überqueren, kreuzen |
| crown | Krone |
| crown jewels | Kronjuwelen |
| cup | Tasse |

## Dd

| | |
|---|---|
| (to) dance | tanzen |
| dancer | Tänzer, Tänzerin |
| danger | Gefahr |
| dark | dunkel |
| daughter | Tochter |
| day | Tag |
| December | Dezember |
| decide | entscheiden |
| department store | Kaufhaus |
| desk | Schreibtisch |

| | | |
|---|---|---|
| | dinner | Abendessen |
| | dinosaur | Dinosaurier |
| | disco | Disco |
| | (to) do | tun, machen |
| | (to) do the washing up | Geschirr spülen |
| | doctor | Arzt |
| | dog | Hund |
| | door | Tür |
| | down | hinunter, senkrecht (Kreuzworträtsel) |
| | dream | Traum |
| | dress | Kleid |
| | (to) drink | trinken |
| | driver's licence | Führerschein |
| | during | während |
| **Ee** | Easter | Ostern |
| | early | früh |
| | (to) eat | essen |
| | egg | Ei |
| | eight | acht |
| | eighth | achter, achte, achtes |
| | eleven | elf |
| | empty | leer |
| | (to) end | beenden |
| | England | England |
| | English | englisch |
| | (to) enjoy | genießen |
| | enough | genug |
| | (to) enter something | etwas betreten |
| | entrance | Eingang |
| | e-mail address | E-Mail-Adresse |
| | eraser | Radiergummi |
| | Excuse me please. | Entschuldigen Sie bitte. |
| | evening | Abend |
| | every | jeder, jede, jedes |
| | exercise book | Schulheft |
| | expensive | teuer |

## Ff

| | |
|---|---|
| (to) fall | fallen |
| family | Familie |
| famous | berühmt |
| fantastic | fantastisch |
| far | weit (weg) |
| farm | Bauernhof |
| fast | schnell |
| father | Vater |
| favourite | Lieblings- |
| (to) feed | füttern |
| felt tip | Filzstift |
| fence | Zaun |
| Ferris wheel | Riesenrad |
| fifteen | fünfzehn |
| fifth | fünfter, fünfte, fünftes |
| (to) find | finden |
| first | erster, erste, erstes |
| fish | Fisch |
| five | fünf |
| February | Februar |
| Friday | Freitag |
| friend | Freund, Freundin |
| flat | Wohnung |
| food | Essen |
| floor | (Fuß)Boden |
| fourth | vierter, vierte, viertes |
| flower | Blume |
| (to) fly | fliegen |
| football | Fußball |
| for | für |
| (to) forget | vergessen |
| fountain | Springbrunnen |
| four | vier |
| France | Frankreich |
| French | französisch |
| from | aus |
| fruit | Obst |
| fun | Spaß |
| funny | lustig |

| | | |
|---|---|---|
| **Gg** | game | Spiel |
| | garage | Garage |
| | garden | Garten |
| | German | deutsch |
| | Germany | Deutschland |
| | geography | Geografie |
| | (to) get | bekommen |
| | (to) get up | aufstehen |
| | girl | Mädchen |
| | (to) give | geben |
| | (to) go | gehen |
| | (to) go shopping | einkaufen gehen |
| | (to) go straight | geradeaus gehen |
| | (to) go swimming | schwimmen gehen |
| | good | gut |
| | grandfather, grandpa | Großvater, Opa |
| | grandmother, grandma | Großmutter, Oma |
| | grandparents | Großeltern |
| | great | großartig, klasse |
| | green | grün |
| | guitar | Gitarre |
| **Hh** | hair | Haar |
| | hand | Hand |
| | handbag | Handtasche |
| | happy | glücklich |
| | Happy birthday! | Herzlichen Glückwunsch zum Geburtstag! |
| | hat | Hut |
| | (to) have (got) | haben, besitzen |
| | (to) have fun | Spaß haben |
| | (to) have to do something | etwas tun müssen |
| | he | er |
| | head | Kopf |
| | Hello! | Hallo! |
| | helmet | Helm |
| | (to) help | helfen |
| | hen | Huhn, Henne |
| | her | ihr, sie |

| | | |
|---|---|---|
| | here | hier |
| | Here you are. | Hier bitte. |
| | him | ihm, ihn |
| | his | sein |
| | history | Geschichte |
| | hobby | Hobby |
| | hockey | (Feld)Hockey |
| | holidays | Ferien |
| | homework | Hausaufgaben |
| | honey | Honig |
| | horse | Pferd |
| | hot | heiß |
| | house | Haus |
| | housework | Hausarbeit |
| | How? | Wie? |
| | How are you? | Wie geht es dir? |
| | How many? | Wie viele? |
| | How much? | Wie viel? |
| | How much is it? | Wie viel kostet es? |
| | husband | Ehemann |
| Ii | I | ich |
| | ice cream | Eiscreme |
| | I'm fine. | Mir geht es gut. |
| | I'm sorry. | Es tut mir leid. |
| | I would like … / I'd like … | Ich hätte gerne … /Ich würde gerne … |
| | in/into | in/in etwas hinein |
| | in front of/in the front | vor/im Vordergrund |
| | information | Information |
| | inside | drinnen, im Innern |
| | interesting | interessant |
| | interview | Interview |
| | (to) interview someone | jemanden interviewen |
| | invitation | Einladung |
| | (to) invite | einladen |
| | it | es |
| Jj | jacket | Jacke |
| | jam | Marmelade |

| | | |
|---|---|---|
| | January | Januar |
| | (to) join something | bei etwas mitmachen |
| | joke | Witz |
| | juice | Saft |
| | July | Juli |
| | June | Juni |
| **Kk** | karate | Karate |
| | kid | Kind |
| | kitchen | Küche |
| | kite | Drachen |
| | (to) know | wissen, kennen |
| **Ll** | lamp | Lampe |
| | language | Sprache |
| | large | groß |
| | lake | See |
| | last | letzter, letzte, letztes |
| | late | spät |
| | later | später |
| | (to) laugh | lachen |
| | (to) learn | lernen |
| | (to) leave | verlassen |
| | leaves | Blätter |
| | left | links |
| | lemonade | Limonade |
| | lesson | Unterrichtsstunde |
| | (to) let | lassen |
| | Let's go! | Lass(t) uns gehen! / Gehen wir! |
| | (to) like | mögen, gernhaben |
| | lion | Löwe |
| | (to) listen to someone/something | jemandem/etwas zuhören, sich etwas anhören |
| | little | klein |
| | (to) live | leben |
| | living room | Wohnzimmer |
| | (to) look | schauen |
| | (to) look for someone/something | nach jemandem/etwas suchen |

| | | |
|---|---|---|
| | (to) look like | aussehen wie |
| | (to) look out of something | aus etwas herausschauen |
| | (to) love | lieben |
| | (to) be lucky | Glück haben |
| | lucky | glücklich |
| | lunch | Mittagessen |
| | lunchtime | Mittagspause |
| **Mm** | man | Mann |
| | many | viele |
| | map | (Straßen)Karte |
| | March | März |
| | market | Markt |
| | match | Spiel (Fußballspiel, Rugbyspiel etc.) |
| | mathematics, maths | Mathematik, Mathe |
| | May | Mai |
| | maybe | vielleicht |
| | me | mir, mich |
| | (to) meet | treffen |
| | middle | Mitte |
| | milk | Milch |
| | minute | Minute |
| | mobile phone | Handy |
| | moment | Moment |
| | Monday | Montag |
| | money | Geld |
| | more | mehr |
| | morning | Morgen |
| | mother | Mutter |
| | mouse, mice | Maus, Mäuse |
| | Mr | Herr |
| | Mrs | Frau |
| | much | viel |
| | mum/mummy | Mama |
| | museum | Museum |
| | music | Musik |
| | must | müssen |
| | my | mein, meine |

| | | |
|---|---|---|
| **Nn** | name | Name |
| | National History Museum | Naturkundemuseum (in London) |
| | national team | Nationalmannschaft |
| | near | nahe, in der Nähe |
| | (to) need | brauchen |
| | nervous | nervös |
| | never | nie, niemals |
| | new | neu |
| | newspaper | Zeitung |
| | next | nächster, nächste, nächstes |
| | next to | neben |
| | nice | nett, schön |
| | nine | neun |
| | ninth | neunter, neunte, neuntes |
| | no | nein |
| | No problem! | Kein Problem! |
| | normally | normalerweise |
| | not | nicht |
| | November | November |
| | now | jetzt |
| **Oo** | October | Oktober |
| | of course | natürlich |
| | often | oft |
| | Oh dear! | Oh mein Gott! |
| | old | alt |
| | on/onto | auf/auf etwas hinauf |
| | one | ein, eine |
| | open | offen |
| | or | oder |
| | orange | Orange |
| | orange juice | Orangensaft |
| | our | unser, unsere |
| | out | aus |
| | outside | draußen |
| | over | vorbei, zu Ende, über |
| | over there | dort drüben |
| | own | eigener, eigene, eigenes |

## Pp

| | |
|---|---|
| packet | Packung, Schachtel |
| (to) paint | malen |
| a pair of (shoes) | ein Paar (Schuhe) |
| palace | Palast |
| parents | Eltern |
| park | Park |
| party | Party |
| (to) pass | (herüber-)reichen, vorbeigehen, vorbeifahren |
| (to) pass a test | einen Test bestehen |
| pavement | Gehweg |
| (to) pay | zahlen, bezahlen |
| PE = physical education | Sport |
| pencil case | Mäppchen |
| people | Leute, Menschen |
| pepper | Pfeffer |
| phone | Telefon |
| phone number | Telefonnummer |
| photo | Foto |
| piano | Klavier |
| picture | Bild |
| (to) pick | pflücken |
| pig | Schwein |
| pink | rosa |
| pizza | Pizza |
| (to) play | spielen |
| player | Spieler, Spielerin |
| plate | Teller |
| please | bitte |
| policeman | Polizist |
| poor | arm |
| postcard | Postkarte |
| poster | Poster |
| (British) pound | (britisches) Pfund (Währung in England) |
| present | Geschenk |
| Prime Minister | Premierminister |
| problem | Problem |
| programme | Programm |

| | | |
|---|---|---|
| | pullover | Pullover |
| | pupil | Schüler, Schülerin |
| | (to) put | setzen, legen, stellen |
| **Qq** | queen | Königin |
| | question | Frage |
| **Rr** | (to) rain | regnen |
| | (to) rake | harken, rechen |
| | RE = religious education | Religion (Fach) |
| | (to) read | lesen |
| | really | wirklich |
| | red | rot |
| | (to) relax | entspannen |
| | restaurant | Restaurant |
| | rich | reich |
| | (to) ride | reiten (Pferd), fahren (Fahrrad, Bus) |
| | (to) ride out | ausreiten |
| | right | richtig, rechts |
| | river | Fluss |
| | road | Straße |
| | roof | Dach |
| | rose | Rose |
| | room | Zimmer |
| | rubbish | Müll |
| | rugby | Rugby |
| | rule | Regel |
| | ruler | Lineal |
| | (to) run | rennen |
| **Ss** | sad | traurig |
| | salt | Salz |
| | sandwich | Sandwich |
| | Saturday | Samstag |
| | sausage | Wurst |
| | (to) say | sagen |
| | school | Schule |
| | school bag | Schultasche |
| | school band | Schulband |

| | |
|---|---|
| school bus | Schulbus |
| school cafeteria | Schulmensa |
| school choir | Schulchor |
| school day | Schultag |
| school team | Schulmannschaft |
| school trip | Schulausflug |
| school newspaper | Schülerzeitung |
| scuba diving | tauchen |
| sea | Meer |
| second | zweiter, zweite, zweites |
| (to) see | sehen |
| September | September |
| (to) set the table | den Tisch decken |
| seven | sieben |
| seventh | siebter, siebte, siebtes |
| she | sie (Einzahl, weiblich) |
| (to) shine | scheinen |
| ship | Schiff |
| shirt | Hemd |
| shoe | Schuh |
| shop | Geschäft |
| shop assistant | Verkäufer, Verkäuferin |
| short | kurz |
| (to) show | zeigen |
| sight | Sehenswürdigkeit |
| sightseeing tour | Stadtrundfahrt |
| silly | dumm, blöd, albern |
| (to) sing | singen |
| singer | Sänger, Sängerin |
| single flight | einfache Fahrt (Riesenrad) |
| sister | Schwester |
| (to) sit | sitzen |
| (to) sit down | sich hinsetzen |
| six | sechs |
| sixth | sechster, sechste, sechstes |
| skirt | Rock |
| slice | Scheibe |
| (to) slip | ausrutschen |
| small | klein |

| | | |
|---|---|---|
| | snowman | Schneemann |
| | sock | Socke |
| | some | etwas, ein paar, einige |
| | something | etwas |
| | sometimes | manchmal |
| | son | Sohn |
| | soon | bald |
| | sorry | Entschuldigung, tut mir leid |
| | southern | südlich |
| | souvenir | Souvenir |
| | Spain | Spanien |
| | (to) speak | sprechen |
| | special | besonders |
| | spoon | Löffel |
| | sport | Sport |
| | spring | Frühling |
| | stadium | Stadion |
| | stamp | Briefmarke |
| | (to) stand up | aufstehen |
| | star | Stern, Star (Popstar, Fußballstar usw.) |
| | (to) start | starten, anfangen, beginnen |
| | station | Bahnhof |
| | (to) stay | bleiben |
| | stall | Stand |
| | still | noch |
| | stone | Stein |
| | street | Straße |
| | style | Stil |
| | subject | Unterrichtsfach |
| | summer | Sommer |
| | sun | Sonne |
| | Sunday | Sonntag |
| | supermarket | Supermarkt |
| | (to) be sure | sich sicher sein |
| | (to) swim | schwimmen |
| | (to) switch off | ausschalten |
| **Tt** | table | Tisch |
| | (to) take | nehmen |

| | |
|---|---|
| (to) take a photo | fotografieren, ein Foto machen |
| (to) take a shower | duschen |
| (to) take the dog for a walk | mit dem Hund Gassi gehen |
| (to) take out | herausnehmen |
| (to) take place | stattfinden |
| Take care! | Pass auf dich auf! |
| (to) talk | reden, sprechen |
| tall | groß |
| taxi | Taxi |
| tea | Tee |
| (to) teach | unterrichten |
| teacher | Lehrer, Lehrerin |
| team | Mannschaft |
| television (TV) | Fernseher |
| (to) tell | sagen, berichten, erzählen |
| ten | zehn |
| tenth | zehnter, zehnte, zehntes |
| tennis | Tennis |
| thank you | danke |
| that | diese(r,s) dort / jener, jene, jenes |
| That's right. | Das ist richtig. |
| theatre | Theater |
| theatre group | Theatergruppe |
| their | ihr, ihrem |
| them | sie (Objekt, Mehrzahl), ihnen |
| there | dort |
| there are | es gibt |
| they | sie (Subjekt, Mehrzahl) |
| these | diese (Mehrzahl) |
| thing | Ding |
| (to) think | denken |
| third | dritter, dritte, drittes |
| this | dies (hier) |
| those | diese dort / jene (Mehrzahl) |
| three | drei |
| through | durch |
| Thursday | Donnerstag |
| ticket | Eintrittskarte |
| tidy | aufgeräumt, ordentlich |

| | | |
|---|---|---|
| | (to) tidy up | aufräumen |
| | time | Zeit |
| | tip | Tipp |
| | tired | müde |
| | toast | Toast |
| | to | zu, nach |
| | today | heute |
| | together | zusammen |
| | tomorrow | morgen |
| | too | auch |
| | on top of | auf der Spitze von |
| | tour | Tour |
| | toy | Spielzeug |
| | town | Stadt |
| | town centre | Stadtzentrum |
| | T-shirt | T-Shirt |
| | train | Zug |
| | training | Training |
| | tree | Baum |
| | Trick or treat! | Süßes oder Saures! (Spruch der Kinder an Halloween) |
| | trip | Ausflug |
| | (to) try | versuchen, ausprobieren |
| | (to) try on | anprobieren |
| | tube | U-Bahn (in London) |
| | Tuesday | Dienstag |
| | turn left | links abbiegen |
| | turn right | rechts abbiegen |
| | twelve | zwölf |
| | twins | Zwillinge |
| | two | zwei |
| **Uu** | umbrella | Regenschirm |
| | uncle | Onkel |
| | under | unter |
| | underground | U-Bahn |
| | (to) understand | verstehen |
| | untidy | unaufgeräumt, unordentlich |

| | | |
|---|---|---|
| | us | uns |
| | usually | gewöhnlicherweise |
| **Vv** | very | sehr |
| | video game | Videospiel |
| | view | Aussicht |
| | village | Dorf |
| | violin | Violine, Geige |
| | (to) visit | besuchen |
| | volleyball | Volleyball |
| **Ww** | (to) wait | warten |
| | walk | Spaziergang |
| | (to) walk | (zu Fuß) gehen |
| | (to) want (to) | wollen, wünschen |
| | warm | warm |
| | warning | Warnung |
| | washing machine | Waschmaschine |
| | (to) watch | beobachten |
| | (to) watch TV | fernsehen |
| | water | Wasser |
| | (to) water | gießen |
| | water skiing | Wasserski |
| | wax | Wachs |
| | waxwork museum | Wachsfigurenmuseum |
| | we | wir |
| | Wednesday | Mittwoch |
| | week | Woche |
| | Well, ... | Gut, ... |
| | wet | nass |
| | wife | Ehefrau |
| | What? | Was? |
| | When? | Wann? |
| | Where? | Wo? |
| | Which? | Welcher? Welche? Welches? |
| | white | weiß |
| | Who? | Wer? |
| | whole | ganz |
| | Why? | Warum? |

| | | |
|---|---|---|
| | (to) wear | tragen (Kleidung) |
| | window | Fenster |
| | windsurfing | Windsurfen |
| | winter | Winter |
| | with | mit |
| | woman | Frau |
| | work | Arbeit |
| | (to) work | arbeiten |
| | world | Welt |
| | (to) write | schreiben |
| | (to) write back | zurückschreiben |
| | wrong | falsch |
| **Yy** | year | Jahr, Jahrgangsstufe (Schule) |
| | yellow | gelb |
| | yesterday | gestern |
| | you | du, ihr (Subjekt, Mehrzahl) |
| | your | dein, deine; Ihr, Ihre; euer, eure |
| | Yours … | Dein …, Deine … (Brief, E-Mail) |
| | youth hostel | Jugendherberge |
| **Zz** | zero | null |
| | zoo | Zoo |

# Key

Dieses Kapitel enthält die Lösungen zu allen Aufgaben. Damit du sie schneller findest, wurden viele der Lösungen **fett hervorgehoben**. Manchmal gibt es oft mehr als nur eine einzige richtige Lösung. Die verschiedenen Lösungsmöglichkeiten sind durch Schrägstriche voneinander getrennt. Die Lösungen zur Textproduktion sind als Vorschlag zu verstehen. Lass dich daher nicht entmutigen, wenn deine Lösung von der im Buch angegebenen abweicht! Prüfe auch deine Rechtschreibung genau. Wenn deine Lösung falsch war, solltest du die Aufgabe später noch einmal wiederholen.

# Topic 1: That's me

**1** **a** Tom is from …

- [ ] Bournemouth.
- [x] Eastbourne.
- [ ] Birmingham.

**b** His name is Tom …

- [ ] Sheldon
- [ ] Sharp
- [x] Shaw

**c** He is …

- [x] eleven years old.
- [ ] ten years old.
- [ ] twelve years old.

**d** His school is …

- [ ] Queen Elizabeth Comprehensive School
- [x] Queen Anne's Comprehensive School
- [ ] Queen Annabel's Comprehensive School

**e** Tom is in …

- [ ] Year 4.
- [ ] Year 6.
- [x] Year 5.

**f** His teacher's name is …

- [ ] Mr Smith.
- [x] Mrs Smith.
- [ ] Mrs Jones.

| | | | right | wrong |
|---|---|---|---|---|
| 2 | a | Catherine is ten years old. | ✓ | |
| | b | She is from London. | | ✓ |
| | c | She lives in Brighton Road. | ✓ | |
| | d | Her e-mail address is Catherine@england.uk. | | ✓ |
| | e | She is in Year 7. | | ✓ |
| | f | There are 25 pupils in her class. | | ✓ |

3 *Lösungsvorschläge:*
- a I am ten years old.
- b You **are 11 years old**.
- c He **is from Eastbourne**.
- d She **is Catherine Smith**.
- e It **is Queen Anne's School**.
- f We **are in Year 5**.
- g You **are from England**.
- h They **are Tom and Catherine**.

4
- a Tom **isn't** from London. He is from Eastbourne.
- b We **aren't** happy about our new teacher. She is not nice.
- c Tom and Catherine **aren't** in Year 6. They are in Year 5.
- d Tom is ill. He **isn't** in school today.
- e Catherine **isn't** in the school bus.
- f It **isn't** a good lesson. It is boring.

5 **Are** you in the theatre group?
Yes, I **am**. **Is** your phone number 23562117?
No, it **isn't**. It is 85720569.
Do you know Catherine? **Is** she nice?
Yes, she **is**.
**Are** Tom and Catherine friends?
Yes, they **are**. **Are** you and Tom in the basketball team?
No, we **aren't**.

6 This is my friend. His **name** is Thomas Shaw. But all his friends call him Tom. He is eleven **years** old and he is **from** Eastbourne. It's a town in England. He lives at 12, High Street. His **phone number** is 01323 812357 and his e-mail

**address** is tom2010@eastbourne.uk. He goes to Queen Anne's Comprehensive School in Eastbourne and he's in **Year** 5. There are 25 **pupils** in his **class**. The name of his class **teacher** is Mrs Smith. Tom's hobbies **are** karate and rugby.

**7** *Beispiel:*
Where are you from? **Munich**
How old are you? **ten years old**
What is your phone number? **6933921**
What is your e-mail address? **daniel.müller@online.de**
What is the name of your school? **Schule am Wiesenweg**
What year are you in? **Year 5**
How many pupils are in your class? **21 pupils**
What's your class teacher's name? **Mrs Huber**

## Topic 2: My friends

**8** TREVOR: "I play in the school band."
"I can speak German."

ZOE: "I like dancing."
"I play hockey in the school team."

**9**

| | | right | wrong |
|---|---|---|---|
| a | Catherine likes Zoe. | ✓ | |
| b | Trevor and Zoe aren't Catherine's best friends. | | ✓ |
| c | Trevor is in the football team. | | ✓ |
| d | He plays the piano, too. | | ✓ |
| e | Trevor's mum is from France. | | ✓ |
| f | Trevor can speak German. | ✓ | |
| g | Zoe likes sports. | ✓ | |
| h | She plays football. | | ✓ |
| i | She is in the school band. | | ✓ |
| j | Zoe isn't a good dancer. | | ✓ |

**10** CATHERINE: **I** am in Year 5. Tom, are **you** in Year 5, too?
TOM: Yes, **I** am in Year 5. Do you know Mrs Smith? Is **she** your teacher?
CATHERINE: Yes, **she** is. Mr Jones, too. **They** are very good teachers.
TOM: What about Trevor? Are **you** friends?
CATHERINE: Yes, **we** are. **He** goes to Queen Anne's School, too.
Are **you** in a school team?
TOM: Yes, **I** am. **I** play rugby.
Are **you** in a school team, too?
CATHERINE: No, **I** am not. **I** sing in the school choir.
TOM: Oh, that's great. Let's go, **we** are late.
CATHERINE: Yes, **you** are right. Let's go!

**11**
- a This is Catherine Smith. **She is/She's** ten years old and lives in Eastbourne.
- b Tom Shaw isn't from London. **He is/He's** from Eastbourne, too.
- c CATHERINE: Tom, how old **are you**?
  TOM: **I am/I'm** eleven years old.
- d This is Trevor and Zoe. **They are/They're** from Queen Anne's School, too.
- e Catherine likes Trevor and Zoe. **They are/They're** her friends.
- f Trevor plays the guitar. **He is/He's** in the school band.
- g Zoe likes singing. **She is/She's** in the school choir.
  **She is/She's** a good dancer, too.
- h TOM: Hi, Catherine and Zoe. **Are you** in Mrs Miller's class?
  CATHERINE and ZOE: No, **we are not/we aren't**. **We are/We're** in Mr Jones's class.

**12**
- a Zoe has got a big **sister**.
- b Trevor and Zoe are in Catherine's **class**.
- c Catherine likes talking to her friends on the **phone**.
- d Zoe's favourite subject is **English**.
- e Trevor likes going to the **cinema**.

**13** *Beispiel:*
My best friend's name **is Tom**.
**He** is from **Eastbourne**.
It is a **town** in **England**.
**Tom is eleven** years old.
His phone **number** is **01323 812357**.

His e-mail **address** is **tom2010@eastbourne.uk**.
My friend's hobbies **are rugby and karate**.
I like my friend because **he is funny and nice**.

## Topic 3: My family

**14**

| | | right | wrong |
|---|---|---|---|
| **a** | Fred and Anita are Catherine's parents. | ☐ | ✓ |
| **b** | Fred and Anita have got three children. | ✓ | ☐ |
| **c** | The Shaws live in a house with a big garden. | ✓ | ☐ |
| **d** | The Shaws have got three dogs. | ☐ | ✓ |
| **e** | Catherine has got two little brothers. | ✓ | ☐ |
| **f** | They are eighteen years old. | ☐ | ✓ |
| **g** | Catherine has got a sister too. | ☐ | ✓ |
| **h** | Catherine and her family live on a big farm. | ☐ | ✓ |

**15**

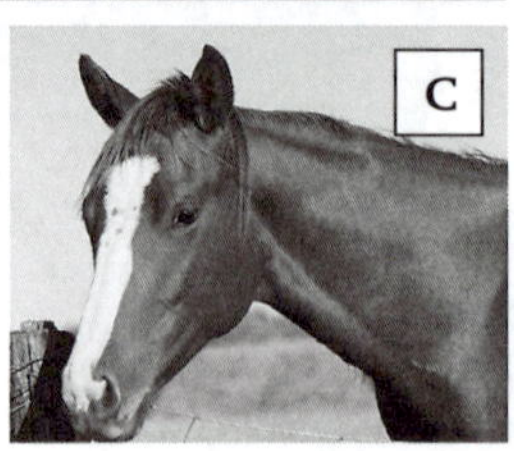

**16**
- **a** Tom **has got** a red bike.
- **b** He **has got** cool new shoes, too.
- **c** We **have got** three cats.
- **d** Susan **has got** a dog.
- **e** Mum and Dad **have got** three children.
- **f** They **have got** a beautiful house.
- **g** The house **has got** a big garden.

**17**
- **a** Catherine **hasn't got/doesn't have** a sister.
- **b** Tom **hasn't got/doesn't have** a dog.
- **c** Tom and his friend Lawrence **haven't got/don't have** a football.
- **d** Catherine **hasn't got/doesn't have** a hamster.
- **e** The Shaws **haven't got/don't have** a blue car.
- **f** Mr and Mrs Smith **haven't got/don't have** a house.
- **g** They **haven't got/don't have** a big garden.
- **h** Catherine's grandmother **hasn't got/doesn't have** ten horses. She has only got one horse.
- **i** Catherine's grandparents **haven't got/don't have** ponies.
- **j** Catherine's grandfather **hasn't got/doesn't have** a dog.

**18**
- **a** Has Tom got two sisters? / Does Tom have two sisters?
  Yes, Tom has (got) two sisters.
- **b** **Have Mr and Mrs Shaw got three children? /**
  **Do Mr and Mrs Shaw have three children?**
  Yes, Mr and Mrs Shaw have (got) three children.
- **c** **Has Becky got a new CD? /**
  **Does Becky have a new CD?**
  Yes, Becky has (got) a new CD.
- **d** **Has Tom got a yellow bike? /**
  **Does Tom have a yellow bike?**
  No, Tom hasn't got/doesn't have a yellow bike.
- **e** **Have Becky and Susan got new shoes? /**
  **Do Becky and Susan have new shoes?**
  No, Becky and Susan haven't got/don't have new shoes.
- **f** **Has Mr Shaw got a new car? /**
  **Does Mr Shaw have a new car?**
  No, Mr Shaw hasn't got/doesn't have a new car.

19

Trevor
sister
cousin
cousin
father
mother
uncle
aunt
grandmother
grandfather

20 John Miller is Trevor's **father**.
He is **38** years old.
Kirsten Miller is Trevor's **mother. She is 37 years old.**
**John and Kirsten are Amy's and Trevor's parents.**
**Amy is Trevor's sister. She is 13 years old.**
**Trevor is Amy's brother. He is 11 years old.**

## Topic 4: My hobbies

21

22 a Tom's favourite hobby is ...

- [ ] cricket.
- [x] rugby.
- [ ] dancing.

b He also likes ...

- [ ] skiing and football.
- [ ] karate and tennis.
- [x] karate and football.

**c** Tom's favourite team is …

- [ ] Arsenal.
- [x] Chelsea.
- [ ] the school team.

**d** Tom doesn't like …

- [x] cricket.
- [ ] karate.
- [ ] tennis.

**e** Tom also plays the …

- [ ] trumpet.
- [ ] drums.
- [x] guitar.

**f** Catherine's favourite hobby is …

- [ ] riding a bike.
- [x] horse riding.
- [ ] playing games.

**g** Jewel is Catherine's …

- [ ] cat.
- [x] horse.
- [ ] friend.

**h** Catherine often helps her grandparents …

- [x] in the garden.
- [ ] in the house.
- [ ] in the kitchen.

**i** Catherine plays …

- [ ] the viola.
- [x] the violin.
- [ ] the guitar.

j Catherine likes the music of …
- ☐ Tokio Hotel.
- ☐ The Friends.
- ☑ Miley Cyrus.

**23**

| | |
|---|---|
| a Tom and Catherine go to Queen Anne's School. | Its name is "The Friends". |
| b Miffy has got a basket. | It's their school. |
| c Trevor is in a band. | It's our hobby. |
| d I love Miley's music. | They are his hobbies. |
| e Tom likes karate and football. | It's her basket. |
| f We love singing. | She's my favourite singer. |

**24**
- a CATHERINE: Look Tom, this is **our** living room.
- b TOM: Oh, **your** living room is big. Is this **your** video game? It's great.
- c CATHERINE: No, it's **my** brother's video game. It's **his** new game.
- d TOM: Here is **your** brother. Hi, Steven!
- e STEVEN: Hi Tom, do you like **my** video game?
- f TOM: Yes, I like it. Let's play **your** game!
- g CATHRINE: Oh no Tom! Let's go and ride **our** bikes.

**25** I play football, I swim/go swimming, I listen to music, I paint, I play table tennis and I read.

**26** *Beispiel:*

Hi **Trevor**,
How are you? What is your favourite hobby?
My **favourite hobby is rugby**. I like it because **it is an exciting sport**.
I also like **karate and football**.
I don't like **cricket** because **it is boring**.
**It is not interesting.**
Write back soon!
**Tom**

## Topic 5: Catherine's room

| | | | right | wrong |
|---|---|---|---|---|
| **27** | a | It's 8.30 in the evening. | ☐ | ☑ |
| | b | Catherine is in the bathroom. | ☐ | ☑ |
| | c | Mrs Smith isn't angry. | ☐ | ☑ |
| | d | Catherine's room is very untidy. | ☑ | ☐ |
| | e | Catherine can't find her green pullover. | ☐ | ☑ |

**28** a Where is Catherine's pullover?

b Catherine wants a …

- ☐ red T-shirt.
- ☑ white T-shirt.
- ☐ yellow T-shirt.

c But she can only have the …

- ☐ red pullover.
- ☐ yellow T-shirt with the white stars.
- ☑ yellow T-shirt with the red stars.

d The white T-shirt is …

- ☐ in the kitchen.
- ☑ in the washing machine.
- ☐ in the living room.

**29** Catherine would like to have …

- **a** an animal.
- **b** a bike.
- **c** a book.
- **d** an ice cream.
- **e** a mobile phone.

**30** Catherine has two brothers, but she doesn't have **a** sister. **The** names of her brothers are David and Steven. Catherine lives with her family in **a** flat, but her grandparents have got **a** house. **The** house is big.
Catherine has got **a** best friend, Zoe. She is **a** very good dancer. **The** two girls, Catherine and Zoe, often go shopping.

**31**

**32** *Beispiele:*

1 I have (got) a brown pair of shoes.
2 I have (got) a black pair of shoes.
3 I have (got) three pairs of trousers.
4 I have (got) a pink skirt.
5 I have (got) a blue jacket.
6 I have (got) four pairs of white socks.
7 I have (got) four pairs of black socks.
8 I have (got) two blue shirts.
9 I have (got) three white T-shirts.
10 I have (got) two pairs of blue jeans.

## Topic 6: Breakfast with the Shaws

**33**

| A | B | C | D | E |
|---|---|---|---|---|
| 6 | 1 | 5 | 3 | 2 |

**34** **a** The Shaw family has an English breakfast on …

- [ ] Mondays.
- [ ] Saturdays.
- [x] Sundays.

**b** An English breakfast has …

- [ ] baked eggs.
- [x] bacon and eggs.
- [ ] chocolate cake.

**c** Mrs Shaw has …

- [ ] two eggs.
- [ ] a cup of toast.
- [x] a slice of toast.

**d** Miffy is a …

- [ ] dog.
- [x] cat.
- [ ] hamster.

**e** What does Mr Shaw like to have?

☐ ☐ ☑

**f** Becky wants to have more …

- ☐ milk.
- ☑ cornflakes.
- ☐ raspberry jam.

**g** Susan wants to have …

- ☐ a slice of toast.
- ☐ beans.
- ☑ cornflakes.

**h** Becky has Susan's …

☑

☐

☐

**35** a Catherine normally has one sandwich for school, but today she has two **sandwiches** in her bag.
b One man is on the bike and two **men** are in the car.
c Tom has one book in his bag and a lot of **books** at home.
d London is a city in England. Munich and Hamburg are **cities** in Germany.
e Mr and Mrs Ratcliffe have one child. Mr and Mrs Shaw have three **children**.
f One woman in the photo has got black hair, the other **women** have got blonde hair.

**36**

**one boy, two boys**

**one house, two houses**

**one girl, two girls**

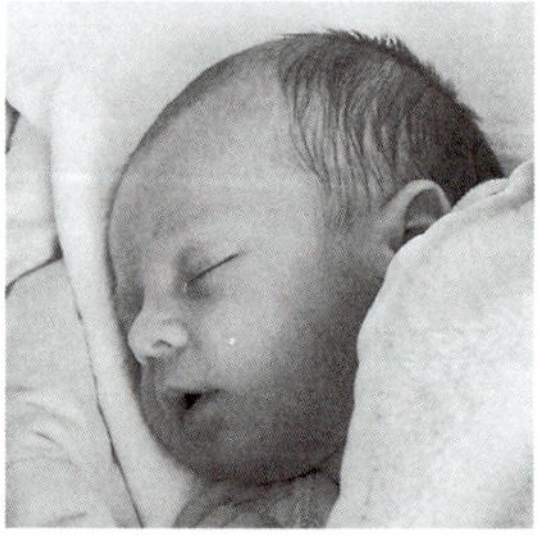

**one baby, two babies**

**one church, two churches**

**one man, two men**

**37**

**38** *Beispiele:*

| Ich esse oder trinke gerne …<br>Ich mag … | Ich esse oder trinke nicht gerne …<br>Ich mag kein(e) … |
|---|---|
| *I like to eat or drink …*<br>*I like …*<br>• *tea*<br>• *fruit*<br>• *toast*<br>• *jam*<br>• *cornflakes*<br>• *orange juice*<br>• … | *I don't like to eat or drink …*<br>*I don't like …*<br>• *coffee*<br>• *apple juice*<br>• *bacon*<br>• *cheese*<br>• *muesli*<br>• *eggs*<br>• … |

## Topic 7: A normal school day

**39**

| 1 | 2 | 3 | 4 | 5 | 6 | 7 | 8 |
|---|---|---|---|---|---|---|---|
| e | h | f | g | a | c | d | b |

**40**
- a Tom gets up at 7 o'clock (7 a.m.).
- b After that he takes a shower and has breakfast.
- c School starts at 9 o'clock (9 a.m.).
- d At 12 o'clock Tom has lunch.
- e School ends at 4 o'clock (4 p.m.).
- f Tom has rugby training on Tuesdays and Thursdays after school.
- g He does his homework and often listens to music.
- h He goes to bed at 9 o'clock (9 p.m.).

**41**
- a Catherine and Zoe **like** biology. It is their favourite subject.
- b Tom **loves** his parents and his sisters.
- c Tom and Trevor **meet** every Saturday.
- d Trevor **speaks** a little bit of German.
- e He always **understands** the teacher's questions.
- f Catherine **does** her homework in the evenings.
- g Catherine **goes** to school first, then she **sees** her grandparents.

**42**
- a On Monday Catherine **goes** horse riding.
- b On **Tuesday** she **sings** in the choir.
- c On **Wednesday she stays** at home and **listens** to music.
- d On **Thursday she has** her violin lesson.
- e On **Friday she meets** Zoe.
- f On **Saturday she helps** her grandparents.
- g On **Sunday she does** something with her family.

**43**
- a Tom **goes** to his rugby training every week.
- b Catherine and Zoe **don't play** football.
- c Zoe **doesn't sing** in a band.
- d David and Steven **don't like** to do their homework.
- e In the summer Steven **eats** ice cream every day.
- f Trevor **doesn't play** the violin.

**44**

**a** Trevor: Do you like being a teacher?
Mrs Smith: Yes, I **do**.

**b** Trevor: **Do** you **have** a dog at home?
Mrs Smith: No, I **don't**, I have a cat. Her name is Kitty.

**c** Trevor: **Does** she **catch** mice?
Mrs Smith: No, she **doesn't**.

**d** Trevor: **Do** you **watch** TV? What is your favourite programme?
Mrs Smith: No, I **don't**. So I don't have a favourite programme.

**e** Trevor: **Do** you **have** a husband?
Mrs Smith: Yes, I **do**. His name is Francis Smith.

**f** Trevor: **Does** he **teach** at a school?
Mrs Smith: No, he **doesn't**. He is a doctor.

**45**

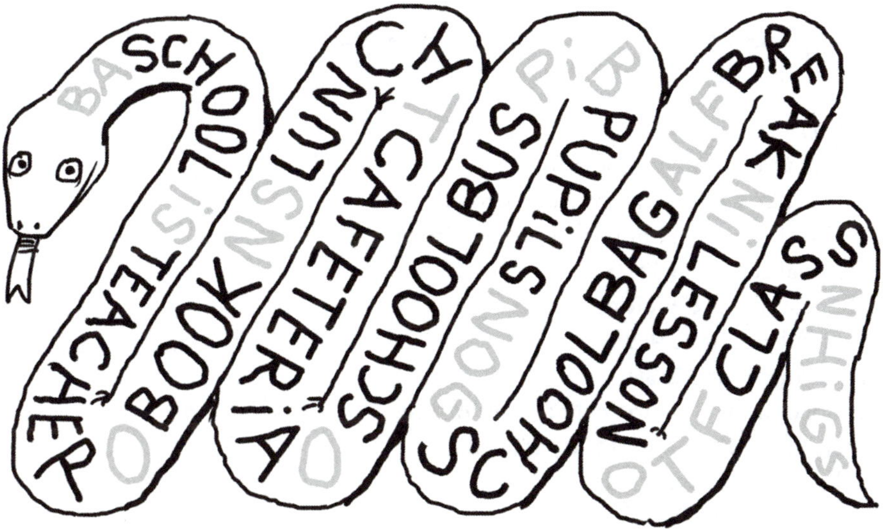

**46**

| Time | Monday | Tuesday | Wednesday | Thursday | Friday |
|---|---|---|---|---|---|
| 08:00 - 08:45 | Maths | Physical Education | Maths | Chemistry | History |
| 08:50 - 09:35 | German | Physical Education | Biology | English | Maths |
| 09:35 - 10:00 | break | break | break | break | break |
| 10:00 - 10:45 | English | German | Music | German | Art |
| 10:50 - 11:35 | Biology | Maths | Chemistry | Maths | Art |
| 11:35 - 12:00 | break | break | break | break | break |
| 12:00 - 12:45 | Biology | English | English | Religious Education | Religious Education |
| 12:50 - 01:35 | Geography | Music | German | History | German |

**47** *Beispiel:*

I get up **at 6:30** in the morning.
Then I **take a shower and have breakfast**.
At **7:30** I leave the house and **go to school**.
I arrive at school **at 7:45**.
School starts **at 8 o'clock**.
My first break is **at 9:35**.
Lunchtime is **at 12:30**.
School ends **at 3 o'clock**. Then I **go home**.
After school I often **meet my friends**.
In the evening I **watch TV**.
I go to bed **at 9 o'clock**.

## Topic 8: At home with the Shaws

**48** **a** Tom's jobs at home:

1. do the washing up
2. take out the rubbish
3. water the flowers
4. tidy up his bedroom

**b** His sisters' jobs:
1. tidy up their bedrooms
2. feed the cat
3. take the family dog for a walk

| | | | right | wrong |
|---|---|---|---|---|
| **49** | **a** | Mr and Mrs Shaw come home early. | ☐ | ☑ |
| | **b** | Becky and Susan don't tidy up their bedrooms. | ☐ | ☑ |
| | **c** | Tom does the washing up after breakfast. | ☐ | ☑ |
| | **d** | In summer Tom often waters the flowers in the garden. | ☑ | ☐ |
| | **e** | Susan always feeds Miffy, the cat. | ☐ | ☑ |
| | **f** | Becky takes the dog for a walk every day. | ☐ | ☑ |
| | **g** | Tom doesn't like housework. | ☑ | ☐ |
| | **h** | Mr Shaw sometimes gives Tom some money. | ☑ | ☐ |
| | **i** | Tom usually buys clothes with the money. | ☐ | ☑ |

**50** **a** Becky helps her parents.
**b** Tom and Trevor buy new CDs.
**c** Becky and Susan tidy up their rooms.
**d** Tom does the washing up.
**e** Tom's father waters the flowers.
**f** Susan feeds the cat.

**51** **a** Tom often helps at home.
**b** Tom and his father usually do the washing up.
**c** Becky always feeds the cat.
**d** Susan takes the dog for a walk every day.
**e** Mr Shaw sometimes gives Tom some money.
**f** Tom usually goes to a music shop.

**52**

1. garden
2. roof
3. garage
4. door
5. window

**53**

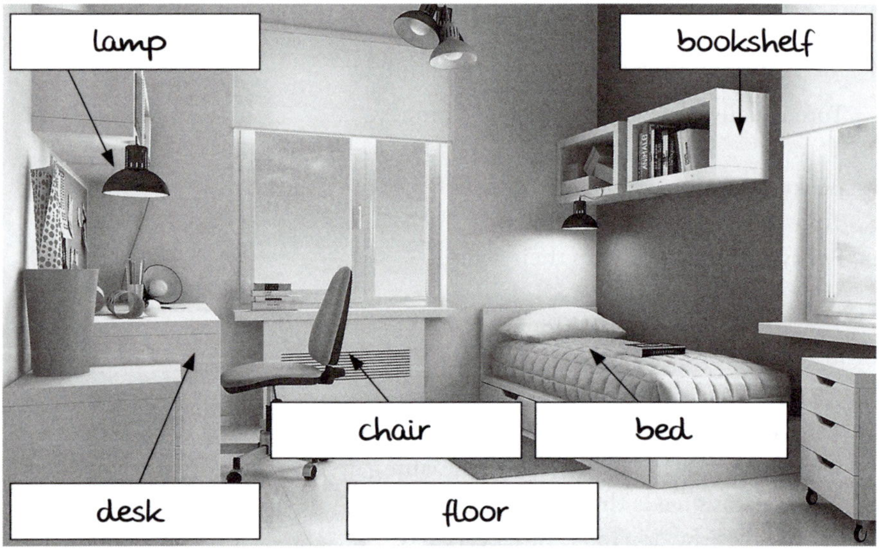

**54**

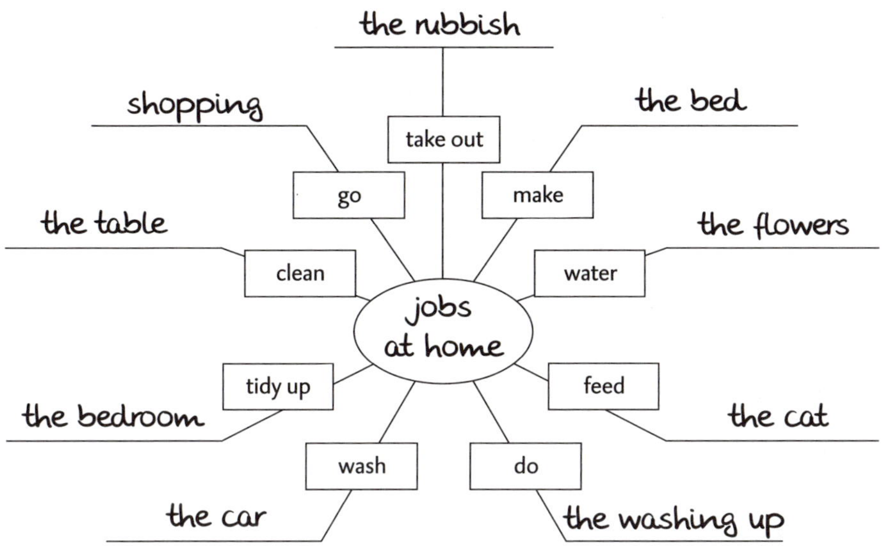


**55**

- **a** Susan has to **help** in the **garden**.
- **b** Tom **has to tidy up** his room.
- **c** Anita **has to buy food**.
- **d** Becky **has to feed the cat**.
- **e** Fred **has to wash the car**.

## Topic 9: At school with Zoe

**56**

| | | right | wrong |
|---|---|---|---|
| **a** | Catherine and her friend Zoe are at home.<br>**Catherine and Zoe are at school/in their classroom.** | ☐ | ✓ |
| **b** | Catherine's school bag is empty.<br>**There are a lot of things in the bag.** | ☐ | ✓ |
| **c** | Catherine can't find her pencil case. | ✓ | ☐ |
| **d** | The pencil case isn't under the desk. | ✓ | ☐ |
| **e** | Catherine's pencil case is blue.<br>**Catherine's pencil case is green.** | ☐ | ✓ |
| **f** | Catherine's pencil case is in her school bag. | ✓ | ☐ |
| **g** | Catherine doesn't like Mrs Ratcliffe.<br>**Catherine likes Mrs Ratcliffe.** | ☐ | ✓ |

**57** a “Hi Catherine, **how** are you? **Why** are you so nervous? What’s wrong with you?”
b “Oh Zoe, I can’t find my pencil case. **Where** is it?”
c “No, Catherine, I don’t have it and I don’t know **where** it is. … **Is** it still in your bag?”
d “That pencil case is blue and **my** pencil case is green.”
e “**Look** in your school bag again. … **There** it is!”
f “But **when** does the next lesson start?”
g “In two **minutes**. **Who** is our new teacher?”

**58** a **What is your name?** My name is Tom.
b **What time is it?** It’s 5 o’clock.
c **What colour is the bike?** The bike is red.
d **What would you like to drink?** I would like to drink an orange juice.
e **What can you see?** I can see a house.

**59** a **Who is in the classroom?** Catherine and Zoe are in the classroom.
b **Who has got a big school bag?** Catherine has got a big school bag.
c **Who is nervous?** Catherine is nervous.
d **Who sits next to Catherine?** Zoe sits next to Catherine.
e **Who always looks for something?**
Catherine always looks for something.
f **Who finds the pencil case?** Zoe finds the pencil case.
g **Who is the new teacher?** Mrs Ratcliffe is the new teacher.

**60** a Where are **the books**? **They are on the table.**
b **Where is Zoe?** She is **in the kitchen.**
c **Where is Trevor? He is in the car.**
d **Where is Tom? He is in the supermarket.**

**61** a How are you?
b How much money have you got? / How much money do you have?
c How many brothers have you got? / How many brothers do you have?
d How old are you?
e How many CDs have you got? / How many CDs do you have?

**62** a Why do you like your birthday? **I like my birthday because** I always get many presents.

- **b** Why are you happy? **I'm happy because** it is my birthday.
- **c** **Why do you walk home?** I walk home because I haven't got a bike.
- **d** Why can't you see the cat? **I can't see the cat because it is** under the table.
- **e** **Why do you like Zoe?** I like Zoe because she is nice.

**63**
- **a** When is school over?
  School is over at 4 o'clock.
- **b** When do you do your homework?
  I do my homework in the afternoon.
- **c** When is your birthday?
  My birthday is in May.
- **d** When is the supermarket open? / When does the supermarket open?
  The supermarket is open at 8 o'clock./ The supermarket opens at 8 o'clock.
- **e** When do you play rugby?
  I play rugby on Thursdays.

**64**
- **a** The pupils are **in** the classroom.
- **b** Jenny sits **next to** her friend Sarah.
- **c** Jenny's schoolbag is **under** the table.
- **d** Sarah's book is **on** the table.
- **e** The teacher's table is **in front of** the blackboard.
- **f** A pupil is **behind** the blackboard.
- **g** The bus stop is **near/next to** the school.

**65** I put my school books in my school bag. Then I put in my exercise books and my pencil case. In my pencil case are pencils, a pen, a ruler, felt-tips, a sharpener and a pair of scissors. I also put in my folder and something to drink.
In the morning my mother gives me a sandwich for break.

## Topic 10: In town

**66** **a** When do Tom, Catherine and their friends meet?

 ☑

 ☐

 ☐

**b** They meet on a …
- ☐ Sunday morning.
- ☑ Saturday morning.
- ☐ Saturday afternoon.

**c** The friends meet …
- ☐ at a computer shop.
- ☑ near the station.
- ☐ near the stadium.

**d** The Lifeboat Museum is about …
- ☐ fish in the sea.
- ☑ ships and the sea.
- ☐ chips and computers.

**e** Who do the friends ask for help?

☐ 

☑ 

☐ 

**f** The Lifeboat Museum is in …
- ☑ King Edward's Parade.
- ☐ Grand Parade.
- ☐ Devonshire Place.

**g** The museum is …
- ☐ boring.
- ☐ funny.
- ☑ interesting.

**h** Tom slips on …

☐ a crab. ☑ a stone. ☐ his shoe.

**67**

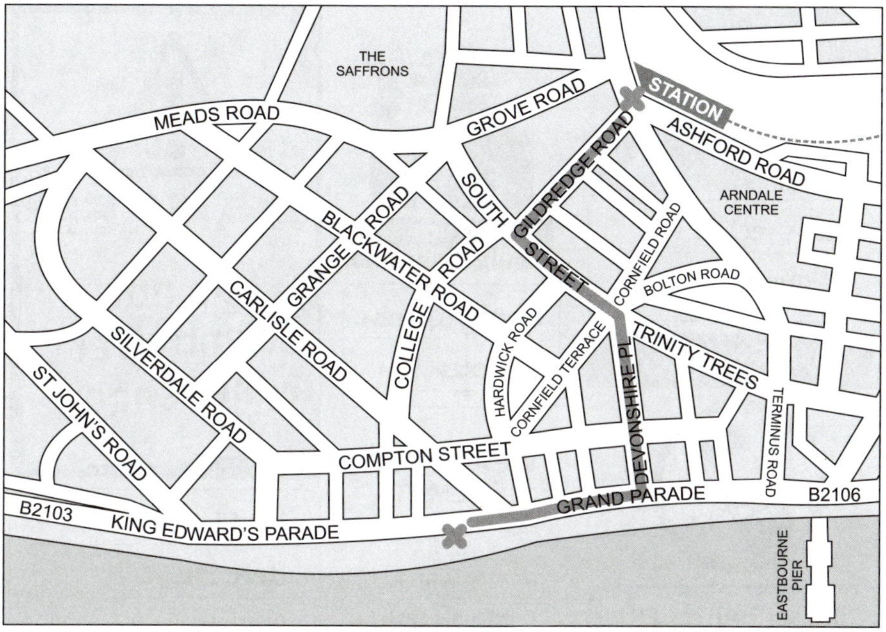


**68**

| | | |
|---|---|---|
| A | I'm fine. | **2** |
| B | Hi, Catherine and Zoe. Let's go to the Lifeboat Museum now. Where is it? | **5** |
| C | Me, too. Where is Trevor? | **3** |
| D | Go along Gildredge Road. Turn left onto South Street. Go straight on. Turn right into Devonshire Place. Then turn right again onto Grand Parade. Go straight on. The Lifeboat Museum is on the left on King Edward's Parade. | **7** |
| E | I don't know. Let's ask the policeman. Excuse me, Sir, where is the Lifeboat Museum? | **6** |
| F | Thank you, Sir. Let's go. | **8** |
| G | Hi, Catherine and Zoe. How are you? | **1** |
| H | He's in the computer shop. But here he is! | **4** |

**69**

Nach rechts schauen!

Bitte alle Handys ausschalten!

Fotografieren verboten!

Tragen Sie Ihren Helm!

Nicht über den Zaun klettern!

**70**

supermarket/
shop
Special offer! 99p
station
cinema
Film today:
market
church
car park

**71** Dear Philipp,
How are **you**? My **name** is Tom Shaw. **I live** in Eastbourne. It is a **town** in England. I would like to **know/learn** more about you and the town you live in. **Do you** live in a **big** town or in a **small** village?
Do you have special sights in your town or village?
Where do you **go** shopping?
Please **write** back soon.
Take care
Tom

## Topic 11: In the countryside

**72**
- a Catherine's grandparents live in a village near Eastbourne.
- b They have twelve hens, a cockerel, three pigs, two cats, a dog and a horse.
- c Sammy is the horse.
- d Catherine helps her grandmother in the garden in spring.
- e She swims in the small lake next to the farm or she rides out with Sammy.
- f She rakes the leaves in autumn.
- g She goes to bed early because it is dark and she is tired.

**73**

| | | right | wrong |
|---|---|---|---|
| a | Catherine's grandparents have got a farm. | ✓ | |
| b | Their house is small. | | ✓ |
| c | They have got two pigs. | | ✓ |
| d | Catherine loves the garden because of the beautiful flowers. | ✓ | |
| e | Catherine never helps her grandfather. | | ✓ |
| f | Sometimes Catherine rides on a horse in summer. | ✓ | |
| g | Catherine never visits her grandparents in winter. | | ✓ |

**74**
- a **Mrs Shaw's** car is pink.
- b **Tom's** computer is new.
- c **Catherine's** friends are nice.
- d **Trevor's** guitar is cool.
- e London is **England's** capital.

**75**
- a This is **Grandma's garden**.
- b This is the **dog's house**.

c This is the **farm's lake**.
d This is **Grandma's and Grandpa's living room**.

**76** a On this day there is no school. The next day is Monday. It's **Sunday**.
b The day after Tuesday is **Wednesday**.
c The day before Saturday is **Friday**.
d It is the fourth day of the week. It's **Thursday**.
e It is the second day of the week. It's **Tuesday**.
f It is the first day of the week. It's **Monday**.
g It is the first day of the weekend. It's **Saturday**.

**77**

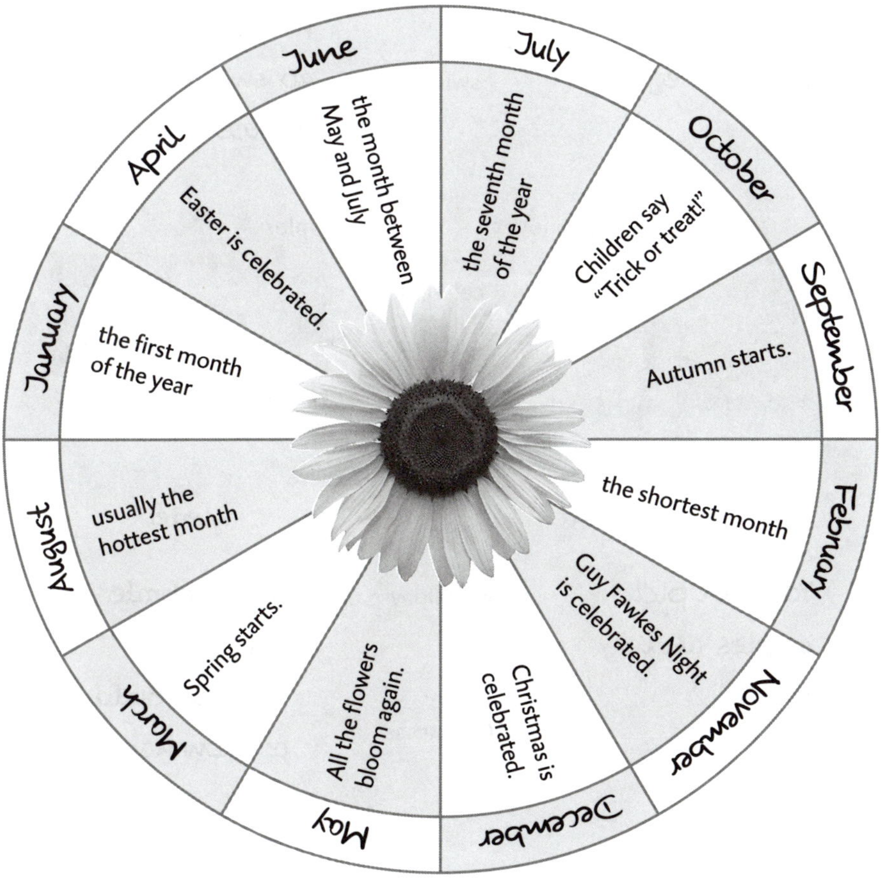

**78**

spring

You can pick flowers and look for Easter eggs.

summer

You can go on holiday. You can go swimming and eat ice cream.

pick
Easter eggs
flowers
fly
ice cream
go
build
swimming
a kite
look for
apples
celebrate
eat
a snowman
on holiday
Christmas

autumn

You can pick apples and fly a kite.

winter

You celebrate Christmas. You can build a snowman.

## Topic 12: The London Eye

79 **a** Tom's class is on a **school trip** to London.

**b** They want to go to ...

- [ ] the Tower of London.
- [x] the London Eye.
- [ ] the London Wheel.

**c** It is a very big Ferris wheel in the centre of the city.

**d** £ **9.50**

**e** They can see the Houses of Parliament, Trafalgar Square, the River Thames, a big boat and Buckingham Palace.

**f** Next Tom wants to go ...

- [ ] to the Houses of Parliament.
- [ ] to Trafalgar Square.
- [x] to Buckingham Palace.

**g** It's the home of ...

- [ ] Queen Elizabeth I.
- [x] Queen Elizabeth II.
- [ ] the British Prime Minister.

80 **a** London is a very **interesting** city.
**b** The class walks through the city on the **first** day of the school trip.
**c** The "London Eye" is a very **big** Ferris wheel.
**d** Tom and his classmates want to have a **beautiful** view of the city.
**e** A flight on the "London Eye" is **expensive**.
**f** At the top of the Ferris wheel they can see a lot of **famous** London sights.
**g** Tom sees a **big** boat on the river.

**81**

**That** is the National Gallery.

**This** is a lion.

**That** is the church St Martin-in-the-Fields.

**This** is a fountain.

**That** is Big Ben.

**This** is Nelson's Column.

82

Those are trees.
These are houses.
PLAZA
Those are buses.
Oxford Circus
Shepherd's Bush 94
Acton Green
159
Marble Arch
LS07 ZUB
N262 PYE
These are taxis.
These are people.

83

Hyde Park
St Paul's Cathedral
The Tower of London
Trafalgar Square
Tower Bridge
Houses of Parliament
Buckingham Palace
London Eye

**84** On the left I can see **the London Eye**. **It is the big Ferris wheel in London.**
On the right **I can see Westminster Abbey**.
In the back **I can see a lot of houses** (**and the sky**).
In the front **I can see the River Thames**.
In the middle **I can see the Houses of Parliament**.

**85** *Lösungsvorschlag:*

Hi Thomas,

When I'm in London I would like to see the Queen. Her home is Buckingham Palace. I would also like to visit London Zoo because I love animals. There are a lot of interesting animals in London Zoo.
I also like David Beckham, the famous football star. I would like to see him at Madame Tussauds as a waxwork.
I would like to visit the large toy shop Hamley's in Regent Street, too. I want to buy something for my little sister there.
I also want to visit the Tower of London to see the Crown Jewels.

Take care and write back soon.

Dennis

## Topic 13: Tom's dream

**86**

| | | right | wrong |
|---|---|---|---|
| **a** | Tom's class will visit Twickenham Football Stadium. | ☐ | ☑ |
| **b** | It's not a very big stadium. | ☐ | ☑ |
| **c** | They will see a match there. | ☐ | ☑ |
| **d** | Tom wants to buy a rugby shirt. | ☑ | ☐ |
| **e** | Jonny Wilkinson is a famous rugby player. | ☑ | ☐ |
| **f** | Tom is a big fan of Jonny Wilkinson. | ☑ | ☐ |
| **g** | Tom doesn't want to be a rugby player. | ☐ | ☑ |

**87** **a** Twickenham Stadium is a stadium for ...

- ☐ 8 200 people.
- ☑ 82 000 people.
- ☐ 820 000 people.

**b** During the stadium tour you can see …

- [x] where the Queen sits.
- [ ] where the reporters sit.
- [ ] where the cameras are.

**c** What does the English team rugby shirt look like?

[ ] [ ] [x]

**d** In the fan shop Trevor sees …

- [ ] a picture of the Queen.
- [ ] Jonny Wilkinson's rugby shirt.
- [x] a poster of Jonny Wilkinson.

**88** **a** I'm sure we **will visit** Twickenham Rugby Stadium tomorrow.
**b** Tom and Trevor **will have fun** in the stadium.
**c** Trevor **will go** with Tom to the fan shop.
**d** The class **won't/will not see** the Queen in the stadium.
**e** Jonny Wilkinson **won't/will not play** in the match today.
**f** Tom **will buy** a rugby shirt.
**g** Tom hopes he **will play** in this stadium one day.
**h** Trevor thinks Tom **won't/will not be** a rugby star.

**89** **a** **Will you** go to London soon, Cathy? – Yes, I will.
**b** **Will it** rain in London? – No, it won't.
**c** Will you be at home next Saturday? – Yes, **I will**.
**d** **Will you** ride on the London Eye? – Yes, I will.
**e** **Will you** see a rugby match? – No, we won't.
**f** Will you visit the Queen? – No, **I / we won't**.
**g** Will she be in London? – No, **she won't**.
**h** Will you buy us a souvenir? – Yes, **I will**.

**90**

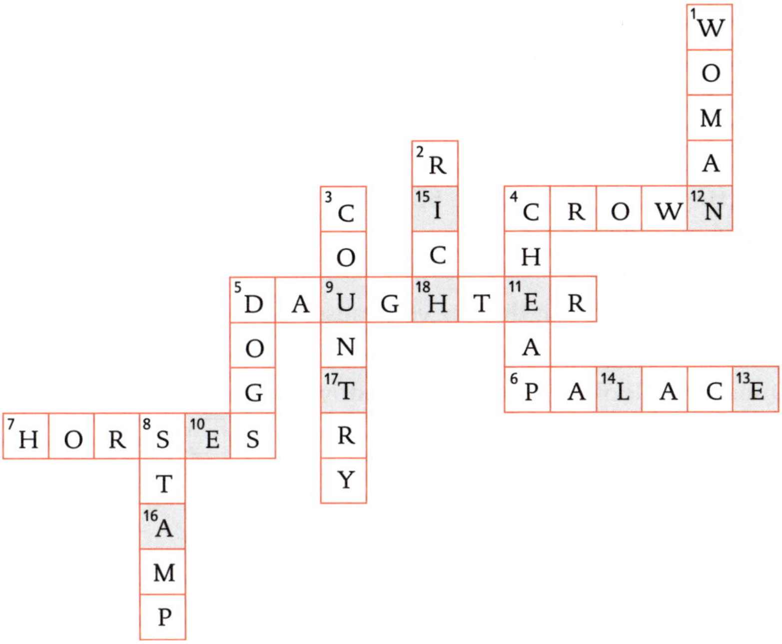


Her name is: Queen Elizabeth II

**91** *Beispiel:*
*name:* Mesut Özil
*birthday:* 15th October 1988
*job:* football player
*What do you know about him/her?*
He comes from Gelsenkirchen, but his parents are from Turkey. He is a very good football player. He plays for Real Madrid with Cristiano Ronaldo and Sami Khedira. He is fast and scores a lot of great goals.
*Why do you like him/her?*
I think he is a very good football player. I want to play for Real Madrid, too.

## Topic 14: A sightseeing tour

**92**
- **a** Tom and his class are going on a **sightseeing tour** through London.
- **b** Tom is sitting next to **Trevor**.
- **c** There are **a lot of people** in front of Madame Tussauds.
- **d** Madame Tussauds is a **waxwork museum**.

e Some **boys** are playing rugby in Regent's Park.
f The queen **lives** in Buckingham Palace.
g **Tom** can't see the Queen.

| 93 | | right | wrong |
|---|---|---|---|
| a | Tom is sitting in the back of the bus.<br>**Tom is sitting in the front of the bus.** | ☐ | ✓ |
| b | Tom is eating a sandwich.<br>**Tom is eating a banana.** | ☐ | ✓ |
| c | A lot of people want to visit the waxwork museum. | ✓ | ☐ |
| d | The Queen is looking out of the window.<br>**The Queen isn't looking out of the window.** | ☐ | ✓ |
| e | The bus is passing Hyde Park.<br>**The bus is passing Regent's Park.** | ☐ | ✓ |
| f | The bus is passing Buckingham Palace. | ✓ | ☐ |

**94**
a Tom **is eating** cornflakes.
b Susan and Vicky **are drinking** milk.
c Trevor **is laughing**.
d The hostel's cat **is playing** with an apple.
e The teachers **are talking** to some pupils.
f It **is raining** outside.
g The bus driver **is waiting** for the pupils.

**95**
a The pupils are **not going** to a restaurant.
They **are going** to a park.
b Susan **is not listening** to Trevor's jokes.
She **is listening** to music.
c Vicky **is not taking** a photo of the Queen.
She **is taking** a photo of Tom.
d Tom **is not buying** a silly hat for his father.
He **is buying** a silly hat for his sister Becky.
e The pupils **are not waiting** for a taxi.
They **are waiting** for the bus.

**96**
a Is Tom looking at a map of London?
b Is Trevor taking a photo of Tom?
c Are the boys playing rugby?
d Is the dog playing with the ball?

**e** Is Trevor telling jokes?
**f** Are we now going back to the youth hostel?

**97**
1. You can buy a **stamp** in a post office.
2. You can eat **fish and chips** in a pub.
3. You can buy a **T-shirt** in Camden **Market**.
4. You can buy a **ticket** for the London tube at an **Underground** station.
5. You can buy **souvenirs** at a souvenir **shop/stall**.

**98**

**A car is crossing** the street.

People **are walking** on the pavement *(Gehweg)*.

A man is **standing in the street**.

People **are waiting** to cross the street.

## Topic 15: Mind the gap!

**99**
- **a** You must look right before you cross a street in London.
- **b** You must mind the gap when you enter the London Underground.
- **c** Don't forget to buy a map.
- **d** You need British pounds to pay in London.
- **e** You must visit the Natural History Museum.
- **f** You must visit Harrods, a very big department store.

**100**
- **a** You often need an umbrella.
- **b** The Changing of the Guard is at 11:30 a.m.
- **c** You can see dinosaurs at the Natural History Museum.
- **d** You can see (all the) famous stars in wax at Madame Tussauds.
- **e** You must write postcards to your best friends.

**101** *Lösungsvorschläge:*
I can speak German.
Trevor can play the piano.
Tom and Catherine can't help me.
Can you help me?
I can help you.

**102**
- **a** In Germany, you **must** be 17 years old to drive a car.
- **b** You **must** be careful when you cross the road in England because the cars come from the right.
- **c** You **can't** visit Buckingham Palace today because it isn't open.
- **d** Jenny **can** play the guitar, but she can't play the piano.

**103**
- **a** You can **take** the London Underground.
- **b** You can **visit** a museum.
- **c** You can **watch** the Changing of the Guard.
- **d** You can **ride** on a red London bus.
- **e** You can **see** the Queen at Madame Tussauds.
- **f** You can **listen** to Big Ben, the clock.
- **g** You can **walk** through London Zoo.
- **h** You can **speak** English in London!

**104** *Beispiel:*
In my town you can do a lot of things: You can visit a cathedral and you must visit the famous History Museum.
Be careful because you must look left first before you cross the road!
You can only pay with Euros and you can't see a queen or a king.

## Topic 16: Zoe's birthday party

**105** **a** Zoe is now …
- [✓] 11 years old.
- [ ] 10 years old.
- [ ] 12 years old.

**b** At the shop she buys things for …
- [ ] her mother's birthday party.
- [✓] her birthday party.
- [ ] her friend's birthday party.

**c** Zoe goes to the shop because …
- [ ] she needs some more presents.
- [✓] she needs some more things for her birthday party.
- [ ] she has to buy something for her mother.

**d** Zoe buys …
- [ ] five bottles of lemonade, four packets of crisps and two boxes of ice cream.
- [ ] five bottles of lemonade, three packets of crisps and four boxes of ice cream.
- [✓] five bottles of lemonade, three packets of crisps and two boxes of ice cream.

**e** She has to pay …
- [✓] £ 11.49.
- [ ] £ 111.49.
- [ ] £ 3.49.

**f** Zoe's friends are already …
- [✓] in front of her house.
- [ ] in front of the shop.
- [ ] inside her house.

g Zoe's friends have ...

☐ a big present for her.
☑ a lot of presents for her.
☐ no present for her.

**106** a The shop is in her street.
b Five bottles of lemonade cost £ 3.99.
c Zoe also buys three pockets of crisps and two boxes of ice cream.
d Zoe has to pay eleven pounds and forty-nine pence (£ 11.49).

**107** a Mr Shaw hasn't got **many** shoes.
b This isn't **much money**.
c There are so **many books**.
d Don't eat so **much chocolate**!
e Tom doesn't drink **much milk**.

**108** SHOP ASSISTANT: Hello, can I help you? What **would you like**?
MARY: I **would like** to buy a dress. **How much is** this dress?
SHOP ASSISTANT: This dress is £ 40.
MARY: Oh. That's too expensive for me. Have you got a cheaper dress?
SHOP ASSISTANT: Yes, I have. Look, these two dresses only cost £ 25.
MARY: Yes, I like those dresses! And the price is OK. I **would like** to try them on.
SHOP ASSISTANT: Do you need **anything else**?
MARY: No, thank you. That's enough for the moment.

**109**

**110**

a The Watsons live on the sixth (6th) floor.
b The Kennedys live **on the second (2nd) floor.**
c The Grahams **live on the fourth (4th) floor.**
d The Penns **live on the ninth (9th) floor.**
e The Parkers **live on the eighth (8th) floor.**
f The O'Gradys **live on the first (1st) floor.**
g The Butchers **live on the third (3rd) floor.**
h The Jennings **live on the fifth (5th) floor.**
i The Scotts **live on the seventh (7th) floor.**
j The Harleys **live on the tenth (10th) floor.**

**111** *Beispiel:*

Things I have to buy:

- crisps
- lemonade
- cake
- chocolate

Things I have to do:

- write invitations
- buy food
- prepare the games
- set the table
- tidy up my room

112 Dear **Catherine**,
I would like to invite you to my **birthday party**.
It takes place on **Wednesday, 13th December**.
It **starts** at **3 o'clock** in the afternoon.
Please **write** me an e-mail or **call/phone** me to tell me if you can come.
See you!
Yours
**Lara**

## Topic 17: Holiday activities

113

| | |
|---|---|
| **Catherine** likes animals, especially her horse, Jewel. She would like to have a painting of Jewel, but doesn't know how to paint. | **Madame Michelle's Arts Camp** |
| **Zoe** loves dancing. When she is older she wants to be a professional dancer and singer. | **Super Dance Academy** |
| **Trevor** would like to speak German better, because he wants to visit his German grandmother, who can't speak English. | **Heinrich Müller Language School** |
| **Tom** likes playing rugby, but during the summer holidays he would like to try out a new sport. | **Fernando's Sports Camp** |

114 **a** Fernando's Sports Camp is for children …
- ☐ from 4 to 18.
- ☑ from 11 to 18.
- ☐ from 10 to 15.

**b** At the sports camp you can do …
- ☑ windsurfing.
- ☐ skiing.
- ☐ sightseeing.

c At the Heinrich Müller Language School you can learn …

- [ ] French.
- [ ] English.
- [x] German.

d In Paris you can climb …

- [x] the Eiffel Tower.
- [ ] Cologne Cathedral.
- [ ] the Louvre.

e The Louvre in Paris is …

- [x] an art museum.
- [ ] a sports museum.
- [ ] a history museum.

f The Super Dance Academy is in …

- [ ] France.
- [x] England.
- [ ] Germany.

g At the Super Dance Academy you can also take …

- [ ] swimming lessons.
- [x] singing lessons.
- [ ] language courses.

115 a This year I **learn** to ski.
Last year I **learned** to paint.

b Yesterday, Tom **watched** the latest Harry Potter film.
He often **watches** a film in the cinema.

c Every year a lot of tourists **visit** Paris.
Last month Catherine **visited** Paris, too.

d Usually I **relax** at home,
but yesterday I **relaxed** on the beach.

e Now I **live** in Eastbourne.
Five years ago I **lived** in London.

f Last week John **played** football, but he usually **plays** tennis.

**116** a TOM: I **went** to Fernando's Sports Camp.
It **was** fun!

b CATHERINE: I **did** painting at Madame Michelle's Arts Camp in Paris.
It **was** fantastic!

c ZOE: I **was** in Liverpool.
I **learned** to dance!

d TREVOR: I **made** a lot of new friends at the language school in Cologne.
Everyone **said** it **was** great!

**117**

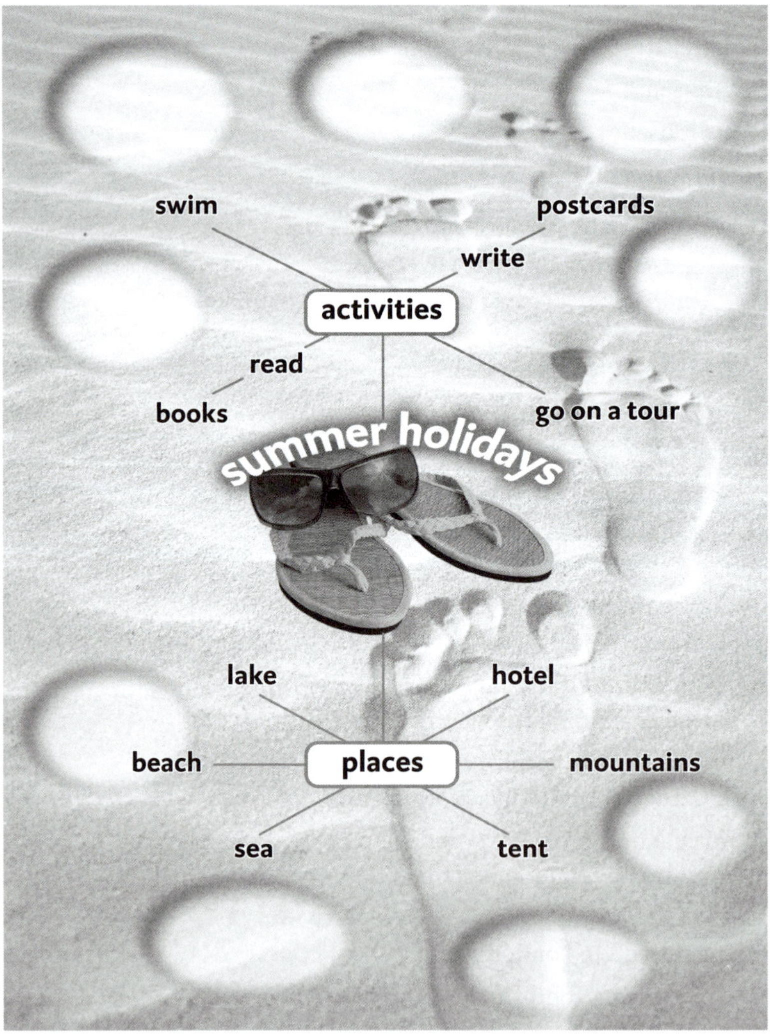

**118** *Beispiel:*

Dear Catherine,

Thank you for your postcard. It must be very nice to live on a farm. I never get up very early in the holidays and I don't like to work.
I am in Paris with my parents. We are doing a lot of sightseeing. Yesterday I went to the top of the Eiffel Tower. That was fantastic! Tomorrow we will visit the Louvre, a famous art museum.
When I come back home I will meet my friends again.

Bye,
Selena

## Bildnachweis

Illustrationen: © Wolf Schröder

S. 1: © Robert Wisdom/Dreamstime.com
S. 2: © Mirobar/Dreamstime.com, © Jacek Chabraszewski/Dreamstime.com
S. 4: © Monkey Business Images/Dreamstime.com
S. 6: © Zentilia/Dreamstime.com
S. 7: © Monika Wisniewska/Dreamstime.com, © Mirobar/Dreamstime.com
S. 9: © Jacek Chabraszewski/Dreamstime.com, © David Davis/Fotolia.com, © Jose Manuel Gelpi Diaz/Dreamstime.com
S. 10: © David Davis/Fotolia.com, © Jose Manuel Gelpi Diaz/Dreamstime.com
S. 12: © Jacek Chabraszewski/Dreamstime.com, © Mirobar/Dreamstime.com, © David Davis/Fotolia.com, © Jose Manuel Gelpi Diaz/Dreamstime.com
S. 13: © Zoom-zoom/Dreamstime.com, © Monkey Business Images/Dreamstime.com, © Jacek Chabraszewski/Dreamstime.com, © http://commons.wikimedia.org/wiki/File:Flag_of_the_United_Kingdom.svg?uselang=de, © Ferenc Szelepcsenyi/Fotolia.com
S. 14: © David Franklin/Dreamstime.com
S. 15: © David Franklin/Dreamstime.com, © Hongqi Zhang/Dreamstime.com, © Wavebreakmedia Ltd/Dreamstime.com, © Monkey Business Images/Dreamstime.com, © Sonya Etchison/Dreamstime.com
S. 16: © Simone Van Den Berg /Dreamstime.com, © Davidgarry/Dreamstime.com, © Rick Hawkins/sxc.hu, © Jyothi/Dreamstime.com, © Rafael Angel Irusta Machin/Dreamstime.com, © Orr Zahavi/Dreamstime.com, © Tina Rencelj/Dreamstime.com
S. 17: © Wavebreakmedia Ltd/Dreamstime.com
S. 20: © Jose Manuel Gelpi Diaz/Dreamstime.com, © Elena Elisseeva/Dreamstime.com, © Katrina Brown/Dreamstime.com, © Monkeybussinessimages/Dreamstime.com, © Multiart61/Dreamstime.com, © bsilvia/Fotolia.com, © Lev Olkha/Dreamstime.com, © Andres Rodriguez/Dreamstime.com,
S. 21: © Monkey Business Images/Dreamstime.com, © Multiart61/Dreamstime.com, © Jose Manuel Gelpi Diaz/Dreamstime.com, © Elena Elisseeva/Dreamstime.com
S. 22: © Jose Manuel Gelpi Diaz/Dreamstime.com, © Dreamstime.com, © Mirobar/Dreamstime.com, © Jacek Chabraszewski/Dreamstime.com
S. 23: © Cybernesco/Dreamstime.com, © Bruce Parrott/Dreamstime.com, © Chucky/Dreamstime.com, © Sergey Goruppa/Dreamstime.com, © Jacek Chabraszewski/Dreamstime.com, © Mirobar/Dreamstime.com, © Katrina Brown/Dreamstime.com, © Vladimir Mucibabic/Dreamstime.com, © Viatcheslav Dusaleev/Dreamstime.com
S. 24: © Vladimir Mucibabic/Dreamstime.com, © Sergey Goruppa/Dreamstime.com, © Dreamzdesigner/Dreamstime.com, © wikimedia commons, © Gemenacom/Dreamstime.com
S. 28: © Annamarinenko/Dreamstime.com, © Jacek Chabraszewski/Dreamstime.com
S. 29: © Simon Krzic/Dreamstime.com, © Lasse Kristensen/Dreamstime.com , © Redaktion
S. 30: © Rob Owen-Wahl/sxc.hu, © Yap Hong Chan/Dreamstime.com, © Feng Yu/Dreamstime.com, © Liddy Hansdottir/Fotolia.com, © Egahen/sxc.hu
S. 31: © Oleksandr Kalyna/Dreamstime.com, © Oleksandr Kalina/Dreamstime.com, © Belliot/Dreamstime.com, © Andrey Armyagov/Dreamstime.com, © Evaletova/Dreamstime.com, Fotograf: Martin Kozák, © http://commons.wikimedia.org/wiki/File:Mens%27_ballroom_shoes,_Eurodance_CZ.jpg, © Edyta Pawlowska/Dreamstime.com
S. 32: © Igor Terekhov/Dreamstime.com
S. 33: © Hongqi Zhang/Dreamstime.com, © Photowitch/Dreamstime.com
S. 34: © Mariia Gerasymenko/Dreamstime.com
S. 35: © Mulltiart61/Dreamstime.com, © Georgii Dolgykh/Dreamstime.com, © Reticent/Dreamstime.com, © Rudchenko/Dreamstime.com
S. 36: ©Tracy Whiteside/Dreamstime.com, © Jyothi/Dreamstime.com, © Zoom-zoom/Dreamstime.com
S. 37: © Marcin Okupniak/Dreamstime.com, © Claude Coquilleau/fotolia.com, © Yuri Arcurs/Fotolia.com, © Olga Nayashkova/Fotolia.com

S. 38: © Guantanamera/Dreamstime.com
S. 42, 108: © Rldcstock/Dreamstime.com
S. 43: © Bruce Parrott/Dreamstime.com, © Gemenacom/Dreamstime.com, © Dreamstime.com, © Alexander Bryljaev/Dreamstime.com, © Liddy Hansdottir/Fotolia.com, © Sergey Goruppa/Dreamstime.com
S. 47: © Irina Ukrainets/Dreamstime.com, © Uwe Mayer/Dreamstime.com, © lusi/sxc.hu, © Monika Wisniewska/Dreamstime.com, © Eric Isselée/Dreamstime.com
S. 49: © Uwe Mayer/Dreamstime.com, © Irina Ukrainets/Dreamstime.com, © Monika Wisniewska/Dreamstime.com
S. 51: © Jyothi/Dreamstime.com, © Annamarinenko/Dreamstime.com
S. 52: © Uwe Mayer/Dreamstime.com, © Maksym Bondarchuk/Dreamstime.com, © Monika Wisniewska/Dreamstime.com, © Irina Ukrainets/Dreamstime.com, © Michal Zacharzewski/sxc.hu
S. 53: © khz/fotolia.com
S. 54: © Gynane/Dreamstime.com, © Maxim Shebeko/Dreamstime.com
S. 57:© Jacek Chabraszewski/Dreamstime.com
S. 58: © Photoeuphoria/Dreamstime.com, © Photodo51/Fotolia.com, © Michal Zacharzewski/sxc.hu, © Barbara Helgason/Dreamstime.com
S. 62: © Nikonas/Dreamstime.com
S. 63: © Davidyoung11111/Dreamstime.com, © Romanchuck/Fotolia.com
S. 64: © Lisa F. Young/Dreamstime.com, © Richard Thomas/Dreamstime.com, © Ron Chapple Studios/Dreamstime.com
S. 66: © Tupungato/Dreamstime.com, © Chetverikoff/Dreamstime.com, © Rainer Hagmayer, © Michel Meynsbrughen/sxc.hu
S. 69: © Davidgarry/Dreamstime.com
S. 71: © Socrates/Dreamstime.com, © Sandra Brunsch/Fotolia.com
S. 72: © Justforever/Dreamstime.com, © Vladislav Gajic/Dreamstime.com
S. 73: © Gautier Willaume-Fotolia.com
S. 74: © Levente Varga/Dreamstime.com, © le-parfait/Fotolia.com, © Treeoflife/Dreamstime.com, © Torsten Wenzler/Dreamstime.com
S. 75: © Fotograf: Diliff, http://commons.wikimedia.org/wiki/File:London_Eye_Jan_2006.jpg, lizenziert unter CC BY-SA 3.0, © Lucian Milasan/Dreamstime.com
S. 78: © Fotograf: Gt-man, http://de.wikipedia.org/w/index.php?title=Datei:Trafalgar_Square.JPG&filetimestamp=20070115200309, lizenziert unter CC-by-sa 2.0/de, © Paul Ransome/Dreamstime.com, © Fotograf: Udo Schoene, http://commons.wikimedia.org/wiki/File:TrafalgarSquare2009.JPG?uselang=de, lizenziert unter CC BY-SA 3.0
S. 79: © Stephen Bures/Dreamstime.com
S. 80: © Peter Lovás/Dreamstime.com, © Bruno Medley /Dreamstime.com, © Mcordell/sxc.hu, © Patrick Wright/Dreamstime.com, © ClaudioDivizia/Dreamstime.com, © Nick Burton/Dreamstime.com, © Shutter1970/Dreamstime.com, © Fotograf: Diliff, http://commons.wikimedia.org/wiki/File:London_Eye_Jan_2006.jpg, lizenziert unter CC BY-SA 3.0
S. 81: © Francocogoli/Dreamstime.com
S. 83: © Kiankhoon/Dreamstime.com, © Fotograf: Jamie Smith, http://de.wikipedia.org/wiki/Datei:TwickersPremFinal08.jpg, lizenziert unter CC BY-SA 3.0
S. 84: © © Patrimonio Designs Limited/Dreamstime.com (Rose)
S. 86: © Sonya Etchison/Dreamstime.com
S. 89: © Fotograf: Citizen59,
http://commons.wikimedia.org/wiki/File:MadameTussaudMuseumLondon.JPG, lizenziert unter CC BY-SA 3.0, © Shutter1970/Dreamstime.com, © Speedfighter17/Dreamstime.com
S. 92: © Mirobar/Dreamstime.com, © Jose Manuel Gelpi Diaz/Dreamstime.com, © Macsim/Dreamstime.com
S. 93: © Peter Lovás/Dreamstime.com

S. 94: © Adrian Gtz/sxc.hu, © Fotograf: Ross, http://commons.wikimedia.org/wiki/File:Edward_VIII_Post_Office,_Bangor_%284%29_-_geograph.org.uk_-_876768.jpg?uselang=de, lizenziert unter CC BY-SA 2.0, © Mihai Blanaru/Dreamstime.com, © Fotograf: GetThePapersGetThePapers, http://commons.wikimedia.org/wiki/File:London-underground-travelcard-2006.jpg, lizenziert unter CC BY-SA 2.5, © Fotograf: Robert Lamb, http://commons.wikimedia.org/wiki/File:The_Camden_Market_-_geograph.org.uk_-_1706856.jpg, lizenziert unter CC BY-SA 2.0, © Fotograf: michael ely, http://commons.wikimedia.org/wiki/File:Fish_and_Chip_Shop,_Beal_Lane,_Shaw_-_geograph.org.uk_-_265547.jpg, lizenziert unter CC BY-SA 2.0, © Janet Hastings/Dreamstime.com, © Paul Jenkinson, © Fotograf: Edwin, http://commons.wikimedia.org/wiki/File:Underground_sign_at_Westminster.jpg
S. 95: © http://commons.wikimedia.org/wiki/File:Oxford.street.london.arp.jpg
S. 96: © Tupungato/Dreamstime.com, © Roland Nagy/Dreamstime.com, © Benis Arapovic/Dreamstime.com, © Fluffthecat/Dreamstime.com, © Dvmsimages/Dreamstime.com, © Jack Rogers/Dreamstime.com , © Fotograf: Marcin Floryan, http://commons.wikimedia.org/wiki/File:Tyrannosaurus_model_at_NHM.jpg, lizenziert unter CC BY-SA 2.5, Harrod's Fotograf: Diliff, http://commons.wikimedia.org/wiki/File:Harrods,_London_-_June_2009.jpg, lizenziert unter CC BY-SA 3.0, © Fotograf: Citizen59, http://commons.wikimedia.org/wiki/File:MadameTussaudMuseumLondon.JPG, lizenziert unter CC BY-SA 3.0, © Yulia Belousova/Dreamstime.com
S. 99: © Dmccale/Dreamstime.com, © Jasmin Krpan/Dreamstime.com, © Shutter1970/Dreamstime.com, © Orhan Çam/Dreamstime.com
S. 101: © Ashestosky/Dreamstime.com, © Nilsz/Dreamstime.com
S. 103: © Nilsz/Dreamstime.com, © Mulltiart61/Dreamstime.com
S. 104: © Fotograf: Martin Kozák; http://commons.wikimedia.org/wiki/File:Mens%27_ballroom_shoes,_Eurodance_CZ.jpg, © Dvmsimages/Dreamstime.com, © Ustyujanin/Dreamstime.com, © Yong hian Lim/Dreamstime.com, © Reticent/Dreamstime.com
S. 105: © Wavebreakmedia Ltd/Dreamstime.com
S. 106: © Andres Rodriguez/Dreamstime.com, © Noam Armonn/Dreamstime.com, © Simon Krzic/Dreamstime.com, © Valua Vitaly/Dreamstime.com, © Thaut Images/Fotolia.com
S. 107: © Stefan Rajewski/Fotolia.com
S. 109: © twixx/Fotolia.com, © Nilsz/Dreamstime.com
S. 110: © Hanns Christoph Merkle/sxc.hu, © Fotograf: Heptagon, http://commons.wikimedia.org/wiki/File:Cologne_cathedral_2.jpg, lizenziert unter CC BY-SA 3.0,
© Diademimages/Dreamstime.com, © Andres Rodriguez/Dreamstime.com
S. 111: © Ines Sulj/Dreamstime.com
S. 115: © Asafta/Dreamstime.com, © Paulwest5/Dreamstime.com
S. 117: © Young Kimpark/Dreamstime.com
S. 137: © Les Cunliffe/Dreamstime.com

*(Bitte blättern Sie um)*